STORAGE
SOLUTIONS

Create a home for everything with
these practical storage ideas

STORAGE
SOLUTIONS

p

This is a Parragon Publishing Book
This edition published in 2004

Parragon Publishing
Queen Street House
4 Queen Street
Bath BA1 1HE
United Kingdom

Copyright © Parragon 2002

Produced by The Bridgewater Book Company Ltd, Lewes, East Sussex

Art Directors Colin Fielder, Sarah Howerd, Michael Whitehead
Editorial Director Fiona Biggs
Editor Sarah Yelling
Photographers Steve Gorton, Alistair Hughes, Steve Tanner

ISBN: 0-75257-166-4

Printed in China

Contents

Introduction

The word "decluttering" is very much part of our vocabulary in this new millennium. There are whole shops devoted to it, and you can actually pay a consultant by the hour to come round to your house and advise you on how to declutter your belongings and put everything away in the correct place. This book, however, shows you how to "declutter" your home yourself—quickly, easily, stylishly, and cheaply—with a selection of practical storage projects that will make tidying up a positive joy at the end of the day. Each room in the house is covered in this book.

ABOVE **Hanging a rail beneath the shelves in a small kitchen will free up a huge amount of cupboard space. Display matching sets of plain-colored crockery for a cool contemporary look, or mismatching flowered or striped tea cups for that country cottage feel.**

The kitchen is a room that people often "live with," because ripping all the units out and starting again can be very expensive, not to mention disruptive. Developments in DIY practices, however, mean that more primers and paint finishes are available than ever before, which means you don't have to live with those beige melamine cupboards! The projects in the Cabinet Makeovers section show you how to change the doors on kitchen units, replace them with slide-out wicker baskets, or even paint them in a zingy color. Nothing is impossible—and you don't even have to think about buying a new kitchen.

Shelves are about as far as some people go on the do-it-yourself front, but even these humble items can be made to look funky and interesting. If you have a yen for a cool modern interior, why not go for the floating shelves? These are simplicity itself to put up and look quite amazing, especially when accessorized with ice-blue walls and silver accessories. Or, if you fancy something a little more traditional, try the adjustable room-height shelving, which can be adapted to any room size. These shelves can all be painted and stained to match your color scheme.

As more and more people choose to work from home, it is becomingly increasingly necessary for a greater divide to exist between home-life clutter and office clutter. The projects detailed here make this easy.

Whether you have a whole room devoted to your work, or just a small understairs space, a portable desk-top unit and a storage unit on castors will prove to be invaluable pieces of equipment. The stylish curved desk will fit into most room schemes, and can be painted in whatever color you like. It is also extremely easy to construct.

So, what are you waiting for? Being neat has never been easier! Take a look round your home, decide what it needs, then pick a project and get making, sewing, or constructing. In this beautifully and clearly photographed book, there are storage solutions to every problem.

ABOVE **An attractive fabric-covered screen will hide television and video equipment in your living room. Use traditional damask or tapestry fabric for a cozy, old-fashioned look, or try fake animal furs and skins for a more modern feel.**

LEFT **A shower caddy quickly becomes indispensable and you'll wonder how you managed without one. Your bathroom will become much tidier, too!**

On The Shelf

Shelves are an indispensable piece of furniture
in any room of the house and because they quickly become colonized with
books, plants, and ornaments, it is wise to put up a good selection. Shelves are
also immensely versatile and can be designed to fit into any room style and
made to match any color scheme. The projects on the following pages describe
a variety of useful shelving solutions, from the ultra-modern floating shelf to
the softer idea of fabric hanging shelves. There is also a handy shelf unit for
the shower, and fabric screens that are used to actually conceal
understairs shelves and storage areas.

Adjustable room-height shelving

You can customize your shelving to suit your individual household requirements with this entirely versatile scheme. Constructed simply from the same wood stock, it can form part of a cladding project, or be fixed directly to a decorated wall surface. Any varnished wood finish can be used to match a room scheme.

If planned and measured accurately, different cleat grids fixed to a wall can serve as a secure base for a variety of projects. Using this grid, a shelving system can run at right angles to the vertical paneling and can perform functional or decorative duties. An advantage is that all wood stock is the same size, 2 x 1in/50 x 25mm, so you can buy in bulk from a lumberyard. The system has been devised to support 5in/127mm-wide shelves, but, if this is too wide, it can easily be revised to accept 4-in/100-mm shelves that will still hold paperbacks and decorative objects. Simply cut

the slot-in shelf supports to 4in/100mm rather than 5in/127mm. Any number of shelf uprights can be incorporated into this versatile scheme, depending on the length of the shelves that will complete the wall. Reckon on one support for every seven TGV uprights, if using 3½-in/90-mm paneling, which gives a support every 25in/630mm. Aim to space out and fix the wall cleats. Plug the wall even if you have bare brick, because of the weight the uprights might have to take. Use number 8 countersunk 2-in/50-mm steel screws, butting short horizontal lengths between the floor to the ceiling shelf-support cleats. All cleats should be 2 x 1in/50 x 25mm, which is the same size as the shelf-support pieces.

Shelving supports

This system employs two sizes of vertical support, screwed to the face of the wall support, creating a gap, into which the horizontal pieces that will support the shelf are slotted. For each upright you will need wood pieces cut from the same stock 5in/127mm-long, positioned starting from flush top, leaving ¾-in/18-mm dividing gaps as you progress down the length. These pieces are secured by center drilling 1½in/38mm from the bottom edge, and screwing through to the upright using 1¼-in/32-mm number 8 (raised) countersunk head brass screws and seatings. A second layer of support pieces is needed only where the shelf supports are to be slotted in; 3-in/76-mm pieces are thus screwed flush with the top of the designated

This versatile adjustable shelving system can be installed on its own or as part of a wall cladding system. It is constructed from simple 2 x 1-in/50 x 25-mm softwood battens. It can be painted or stained in your chosen colors.

5-in/127-mm pieces by center drilling 1½in/38mm from the bottom edge in exactly the same way as before. Slot in the shelf support horizontals, which are also 5-in/127-mm pieces, to check the fit in the slot and to see if they hold a spirit-levelled shelf correctly. When you are happy with everything, sand all the pieces lightly to remove sharp edges and any splinters. For added strength, you can glue as well as screw the pieces together.

Finishing the wall

Now that the shelving system is complete, invisibly pin the TGV uprights to the horizontal cleats. Seven should fit snugly between the uprights. File the wood to fit the wall edges. The join at the TGV can be expanded slightly to take up a minor shortfall. The wood can be varnished with the finish of your choice, as can the shelving uprights and support pieces, and a baseboard added if desired.

STEP 1 Lay out the 5in/127mm-long pieces of wood on the wall support cleat. It is advisable to space them with the shelf cleats in order to ensure a tight fit.

STEP 2 The next stage is to clamp and then screw the sections of lumber to the support batten. For this you should use countersunk-head brass screws and screw seats.

STEP 3 Attach the 3-in/76-mm lengths of cleat to the first lengths in the same manner, flush with the top edge. You should use countersunk-head brass screws and seats as before.

STEP 4 Finally, check the fit of the shelf support battens in their slots. It is important that the fit is exact; if the shelf supports are loose, the shelf will not be stable.

YOU WILL NEED:
- FLOATING SHELF
  PACK—INCLUDING
  SPECIAL FITTINGS,
  SCREWS, AND WALL
  ANCHORS
- TAPE MEASURE/
  LONG RULER
- STRAIGHT EDGE WITH
  BUILT-IN SPIRIT LEVEL
- PENCIL
- DRILL
- CORRECT DRILL BIT
  FOR YOUR WALL,
  I.E. MASONRY OR
  PLASTERBOARD

PROJECT TWO

Floating shelves

The essence of the cool, minimalist style is that rooms should appear to be emptier than they actually are. Create the impression of open space by fitting shelving that seems to float in the air without any visible support system. There are several different systems on the market that work very efficiently, so instead of "re-inventing the wheel" the project shows how to use one of the existing designs. Choose a length to suit the proportions of your walls and the things you wish to display, as it is important to keep to the open, uncluttered style.

These simple shelves seem to float in space. They blend in well with a minimalist decorating scheme.

HOW TO DO IT

Simple to fit and a minimalist's dream, these shelves are magical. But, as with most tricks, the explanation is quite simple.

STEP 1 Having decided on the best position for the shelf, measure and mark it on the wall lightly in pencil.

STEP 2 Hold the support up to the wall and check it with the spirit level.

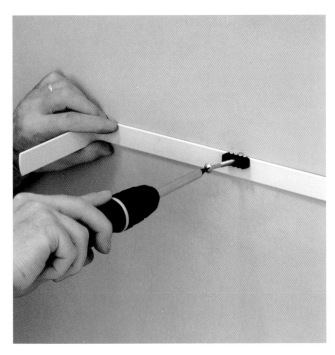

STEP 3 Mark the fixing positions for the supports then remove them and drill and anchor the wall.

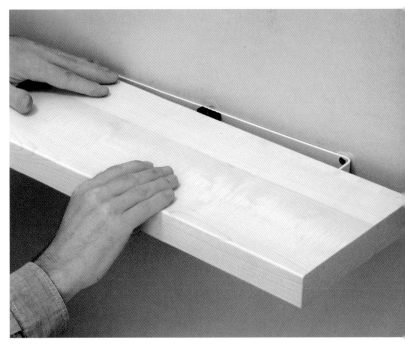

STEP 4 Fix the shelf on to the wall supports.

YOU WILL NEED:

- WOODEN BATTEN,
  ½IN/12MM THICK,
  25MM/1IN WIDE
- SEW-ON, TOUCH-AND-
  CLOSE TAPE
- STAPLE GUN
- TAPE MEASURE
- LENGTH OF
  PATTERNED FABRIC
- LENGTH OF
  PLAIN FABRIC
- NEEDLE AND THREAD
- SEWING MACHINE
- METAL EYELETS
- EYELET PLIERS
- AIR-ERASABLE PEN
- CUP HOOKS
- PINS
- SCISSORS
- STEAM IRON

PROJECT THREE

Shelving hideaways

Most of us have areas in the home that would benefit from being kept hidden—an alcove of dishevelled books or a bathroom shelving unit full of mismatched toiletries.

Luckily these can be concealed from view behind fabric blinds or screens. A Roman or roller blind is great for hiding all sorts of clutter, and you can just draw it up for access.

Shelving hideaways can be used to conceal a multitude of things. Use fabric that holds its shape well.

HOW TO DO IT

Make this smart cover to hang in front of an open cupboard, alcove, or shelving unit. The cover is hung from a wooden batten fixed to the upper edge, and a row of eyelets along the side edges is slipped onto hooks so the cover can be held open at different levels. The cover has a contrast lining, so it is reversible to ring the changes and can be hooked open to reveal the underside.

STEP 1 Fix a ½in/12mm-thick, 1in/25mm-wide wooden batten to the upper edge of the open area. It should extend at least 1in/25mm on each side of the open area. Staple the stiff section of sew-on, touch-and-close tape to the batten. Measure the length of the batten and the drop of the cover from the top of the batten. For the cover, cut one rectangle or square of the main fabric and one of contrast fabric that is the length of the batten plus 1¼in/32mm by the drop plus 1¼in/32mm.

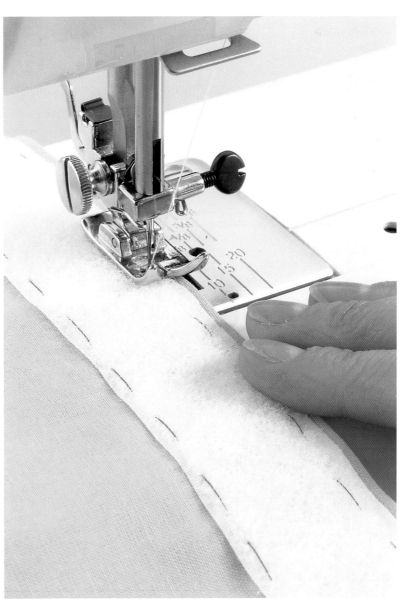

STEP 2 With the right sides facing, stitch the covers together, taking a ⅝-in/15-mm seam allowance and leaving a gap to turn on the upper edge. Clip the corners, turn right side out, and press.

STEP 3 Baste and stitch the corresponding length of touch-and-close tape to the upper edge of the cover.

STEP 4 Following the manufacturer's instructions, fix a ⅝-in/15-mm diameter metal eyelet ¾in/20mm within the lower corners. Use an air-erasable pen to mark eyelet positions ¾in/20mm within the side edges approximately 9in/230mm apart. Fix the eyelets in place with the eyelet pliers. Press the cover onto the batten. Fix cup hooks to the wall or wood surround under each eyelet.

YOU WILL NEED:

- VARIOUS
  ABRASIVE PAPERS
- SANDING BLOCK
- SCREWDRIVER
- WHITE LIMING WAX
- CLEAR WAX
- COLORED
  PIGMENTS
- FINE STEEL WOOL
- POLISHING CLOTH
- WOOD GLUE

PROJECT FOUR

Kitchen shelves

An old self-assembly pine unit that had fallen apart and been thrown in a skip provided a perfect set of surfaces for subtle waxed finishes, each one looking as if it were reflecting a different colored light into the room—a great improvement on the original finish.

STEP 1 The unit was loosely re-assembled, and the original surface removed using medium grade, followed by fine grade, wet silicon carbide abrasive paper.

STEP 2 The finish residue was removed from the dowel holes using an old screwdriver, and the surface sanded using 240 grit aluminum oxide wrapped around a sanding block.

STEP 3 Clear wax mixed with color pigment was rubbed into the grain with fine steel wool.

STEP 4 The waxed surfaces were polished to a fine sheen using a soft, lint-free cloth.

STEP 5 Wood glue was run into the dowel holes, prior to re-insertion of the fluted dowels.

STEP 6 Re-assembly—the different color-waxed shelves were glued to the other half of the dowels.

YOU WILL NEED:
• CLOSELY WOVEN
  FABRIC—SUCH AS
  CALICO, DENIM,
  OR CANVAS
• NEEDLE AND THREAD
• SEWING MACHINE
• TAILOR'S CHALK
• LONG RULE
• PINS
• CORRUGATED
  CARDBOARD
• SEW-ON,
  TOUCH-AND-CLOSE
  TAPE
• SCISSORS
• STEAM IRON
• 3 METAL PAPER
  FASTENERS

PROJECT FIVE

Hanging shelves

A set of sturdy fabric hanging shelves is great for storing T-shirts and knitwear. The shelves are applied to a closet rail with a hanging strap that fastens with touch-and-close tape. The shelves are reinforced with corrugated cardboard and are very lightweight.

Use a colorful, striped canvas to make this useful set of hanging shelves. Remember to position the stripes centrally when cutting out the fabric pieces.

HOW TO DO IT

8⅝in/221mm	8⅝in/221mm	8⅝in/221mm	8⅝in/221mm

HEMMED EDGE

HEMMED EDGE

Use this diagram to cut out the fabric for your hanging shelves. Draw lines in tailor's chalk as indicated to divide the piece of fabric into four equal sections.

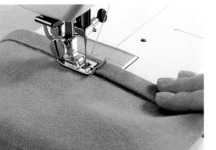

STEP 1 Refer to the diagram to cut a rectangle of fabric for the support 3ft 2¾in x 2ft 10¾in/980 x 885mm. Press ⅜in/10mm under, then ⅝in/15mm on the short edges. Stitch close to the inner pressed edges.

STEP 2 Cut three shelves from fabric 24½ x 12¼in/623 x 310mm. With the wrong sides facing, press the shelves widthwise in half and topstitch ¼in/6mm from the pressed edges; these will be the front edges. Pin the opposite raw edges together; these will be at the back of the shelves.

STEP 3 Draw the lines on the wrong side of the support using tailor's chalk. With the underside of the shelves facing the support, pin the back edge of the shelves along the lines, matching the centers.

STEP 4 Baste the shelves in place. Cut five 10¾-in/275-mm squares of corrugated cardboard. Slip one square centrally inside the middle shelf. Pin the raw edges together to enclose the cardboard.

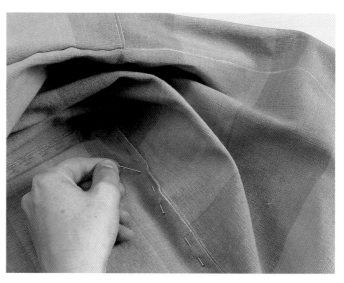

STEP 5 Fold the support around each side of the middle shelf, matching the raw edges to the drawn lines. Pin and baste the side edges of the shelves to the support. Insert a square of cardboard into the remaining shelves, and pin and baste them to the support in the same way.

STEP 6 Fold the support along the lines at the back of the shelves, enclosing the raw shelf edges. Pin and stitch the back edge, taking a ¼-in/6-mm seam allowance, and starting and finishing ¼in/6mm from the side edges of the shelves. Fold the support along the lines at the sides of the shelves, enclosing the raw shelf edges. Pin and stitch the side edges, taking a ¼-in/6-mm seam allowance, starting at the back seam and continuing to the front hemmed edges.

STEP 7 Cut a rectangle of fabric for the hanging strap 11½ x 8in/293 x 200mm. Press ¼in/6mm under, then ⅜in/10mm on the short edges. Stitch close to the inner edges. Press ⅜in/10mm under on one long edge. Pin and stitch one section of sew-on, touch-and-close tape on top. Press ⅜in/10mm under on the right side on the other long edge. Pin and stitch the other section of touch-and-close tape on top.

STEP 8 Cut two rectangles of fabric 2ft 1¼in x 13in/642 x 330mm for the roof and base. Mark widthwise across the center of the roof with pins. Pin the hanging strap centrally to one half of the roof, with the right sides facing and the long edges of the strap parallel to the center line. Stitch the strap to the roof ½in/12mm each side of the center of the strap. Remove the pins.

STEP 9 With the right sides facing, fold the roof and base widthwise in half. Stitch the short edges, taking a ⅜-in/10-mm seam allowance. Clip the corners, turn right side out, and press. Topstitch ¼in/6mm from the pressed edges; these will be the front edges. Slip a cardboard square inside. Secure the roof layers together with three metal paper fasteners along the center of the strap. With the top of the roof facing the right side of the back of the support, stitch the roof centrally to the upper edge, taking a ⅜-in/10-mm seam allowance. Stitch the base to the lower edge in the same way. Clip the seam allowance diagonally at the end of the seam on the roof and base .

STEP 10 Press ⅜in/10mm under on the raw edges of the support. Fold the roof and base over the seams. Stitch the back edge 5/16in/8mm from the seam, starting and finishing 5/16in/8mm inside the side edges. Pin the pressed edges and sides of the roof together. Stitch close to the outer edges. Stitch ¼in/6mm inside the edges, starting 5/16in/8mm from the back edge. Repeat for the base.

PROJECT SIX
Shower caddy

Trying to locate the soap, shampoo, or sponge can be highly frustrating when water is cascading into your eyes. This simple solution should help to keep everything you need in one place, close to hand when you need it. It is ideally suited to a tiled wall, and its beauty lies in the fact that only two holes are drilled through the tiling, with the rest going into the wooden support.

YOU WILL NEED:
- A NICE PLANK OF WOOD, ABOUT 20 x 4IN/500 x 100MM. DRIFTWOOD IS IDEAL, BUT NEW WOOD WITH AN INTERESTING GRAIN, SUCH AS AN OFF-CUT OF PARANÁ PINE OR A FRUIT WOOD, WOULD ALSO LOOK GOOD. ASK A LUMBER MERCHANT WHAT SUITABLE OFF-CUTS THEY HAVE, EXPLAINING THE USE IT WILL BE PUT TO. YOU MAY ALSO LIKE TO STAIN AND VARNISH THE WOOD.
- SOAP DISH
- COAT HOOK
- DRILL
- 3/8-IN/10-MM TILE BIT
- PAINTER'S TAPE
- PENCIL
- SPIRIT LEVEL
- NON-RUSTING SCREWS TO ATTACH COAT HOOK (SHOULD COME WITH SCREWS)
- 2 x 3-IN/75-MM No. 10 SCREWS TO FIX THE WOOD TO THE TILED WALL (THE SCREW LENGTH DEPENDS UPON THE DEPTH OF YOUR WOOD)
- WALL ANCHORS
- BRASS CUPPED SCREWS
- BRADAWL

This shower caddy lets you have a range of fittings with only two holes drilled through the tiles. All the rest are drilled to the wooden caddy.

HOW TO DO IT

STEP 1 Find the ideal position for the caddy on the shower wall, making quite sure that there are no pipes behind the tiles where the screws will be located! Mark the positions for the components and the shelf.

STEP 2 Drill two evenly spaced holes in the shelf end.

STEP 3 Screw the top shelf to the back plank using brass cupped screws. Screw the coat hook and soap dish into position.

STEP 4 Place the unit in position on the wall. Mark through the pre-drilled holes onto the wall using a bradawl.

STEP 5 Drill holes through the tiles using the painter's tape to stop the tile bit from skidding. Insert wall anchors.

STEP 6 Screw the unit to the wall using the brass cupped screws.

Storage box sections

Whether you need to reinforce sagging shelves with vertical supports or make up a self-supporting unit with stepped sides, the same simple wood joint can be used. Halving joints let the shelves slot together at right angles, forming a strong, unseen bond, which can also be a decorative feature.

Weight for support

Shelving systems, constructed from 1-in/25-mm boards or ¾-in/18-mm plywood machined to size, are ideal for fixing in an alcove. The recess will generally be less than 6ft/1.8m-wide and the shelf length, if supported on cleats to the side and rear, will be perfectly stable. Longer lengths, needed to span a gap where, say, two rooms have been knocked into one and the resultant distance between chimney breasts is over 10ft/3m, are liable to sag, particularly if they are 12in/300mm in width. Front

A modular box-section storage system can provide a versatile means of containing and displaying a wide variety of domestic objects. Such systems can be tailored to meet your specific needs.

support pieces, glued and screwed under and flush with the front edge of each shelf, will help, but very heavy weights will still cause problems.

It is reasonable to assume that a long, wide shelf will be used to hold larger, heavier items than a small shelf, so it must be constructed with more support. Load-bearing shelves can have brackets screwed underneath, either as separate fixed items or as part of an adjustable shelving system, where removable brackets are slotted into steel uprights screwed to the wall. There are numerous adjustable systems on the market, all using the same principle, and the heavy-duty ones are very strong indeed. The wall fixings must involve no less than 2¼-in/56-mm number 10 countersunk screws driven into heavy-duty wall plugs. The uprights should be spaced 2½ft/750mm apart. Heavy-duty adjustable shelving is available in only very basic colors, however. Although you can paint it yourself, and it may look effective in a workroom, garage, or outbuilding, it isn't exactly subtle. There is a better, much more attractive loadbearing support system for a living area, which you can construct yourself.

A self-supporting box system

This is a simple wooden unit that relies on horizontal and vertical boards meeting at a series of halving joints and providing mutual support. A halving joint is simple to cut and, when accurate, extremely strong and virtually invisible. The principle behind halving joints (also called half-and-half joints or half-laps) is that where the timbers meet or overlap at right-angles, one exact half of each piece is cut and removed to allow the pieces to slot together. The

STEP 1 Cut the first half of the joint in one board. You can subsequently use it as a template to mark the matching half with your marking knife.

STEP 2 Cut the joint by making a series of saw cuts through the waste to the bottom of each of the slots. Then remove the waste with a thin chisel.

STEP 3 Then check the fit of each of the joints. They should all be snug, and making saw cuts on the waste side of each marked line should ensure this.

STEP 4 Glue inside the housings of the corresponding joint halves and carefully assemble the boards.

STEP 5 Clamp and wipe off glue. The unit can be strengthened by gluing and pinning on a plywood backing.

wood can be clamped securely, marked out with a knife, and cut together so that the housings are the same width as the thickness of the wood, and cut back with a chisel to a shoulder half the width of the timber. Always saw on the waste side of the marked line when cutting halving joints. If you don't, the housings will be too wide by the width of the saw blade, and the joint will be loose.

Custom building

Any size of unit can be constructed in this way, depending on your storage requirements, and the space available. A drawing dividing the wall space into compartments is a good start. These can be any size, but square is easy and uniformly attractive. Consider using measurements that turn the unit into a series of cubes: if your chosen wood is 1ft/300mm wide, use the same figure for the internal dimensions of each box. A scaled-down model made of cardboard will give you a better idea of how it will look—slots cut in the cardboard will join together in exactly the same way as the wood. The top of the unit need not reach the ceiling. A long top shelf for houseplants and ornaments is created by forming external corners, which are simply one-sided halving joints. Your unit is floor-standing, so you need to consider a plinth for the base, and this should be the height of the baseboard. Flush at the front and sides, the plinth can be set forward the width of the skirting at the back of the base, so that the unit back is flush with the wall.

Securing and backing

If you are making a small unit, clamping it square as you glue the joints will ensure it is stable enough. Larger units can be glued in sections as you proceed, but any "play" in the halving joints will result in undue pressure being placed on the unit's square corners. A support cleat glued and screwed under the top back edge of each top corner box will hold that corner square, and allow you to drill through and fix the unit to the wall. If you prefer, you can attach a back panel, placing the unit face-down, and confirming that it is square.

Cut ¼-in/6-mm plywood to fit the outside back, and glue and pin into position with brads. Make sure that the best side of the plywood is visible from the front. The unit is now stable and free-standing. Screws driven through the backing into the wall can be used to provide extra security, if required.

Hang-Ups

Hanging things up and out of the way can minimize
clutter amazingly, and make for a much tidier home. A smart peg rail, for
example, makes sure that coats and hats have a permanent home all year round,
while a slick chrome rod in the kitchen gets utensils out and within easy reach,
freeing up vital drawer space. A shelf above a rail is particularly useful in
a child's bedroom; toys can be stored on the shelf, while bags of bricks and
figures can hang neatly from the pegs below. A softwood pinboard is a fun
accessory in teenagers' rooms, allowing them to stick up those
essential phone numbers and study lists.

YOU WILL NEED:
- 2 x 1-IN/50 x 25-MM PAR (PLANED ALL ROUND) LUMBER, THE LENGTH OF YOUR WALL
- WOODEN PEGS OR 6FT/2M OF 1-IN/25-MM DOWEL
- 1-IN/25-MM SPADE BIT
- DRILL
- MEDIUM GRADE SANDPAPER
- WOOD GLUE
- STRAIGHT EDGE WITH BUILT-IN SPIRIT LEVEL
- TAPE MEASURE
- PENCIL
- WALL ANCHORS
- NO. 6 MASONRY AND A COUNTERSINK BIT AND A 6-MM CLEARANCE BIT
- 1¼-IN/32-MM No. 8 COUNTERSINK SCREWS FOR FIXINGS
- WOOD FILLER
- PRIMER
- SHAKER BLUE PAINT
- PAINT BRUSH

PROJECT ONE

A Shaker-style peg rail

The Shakers were a religious group who lived communally. They needed plenty of clear floor space for their meetings so they hung their chairs from rails on the wall. The Shakers are famous for their simple but beautifully crafted furniture, much of which was "built in" to keep the rooms plain-looking, although they found ways of adding decorative touches without breaking the religion's strict guidelines on ornament. Shaker style has become very popular in the past decade and fits in very well with the modern trend for decluttering.

A brightly colored peg rail is useful in any room of the house. Children's rooms will benefit the most from an arrangement like this one.

HOW TO DO IT

Peg rails can be positioned at the most useful height for any room – up high in the bathroom or low down in a child's bedroom.

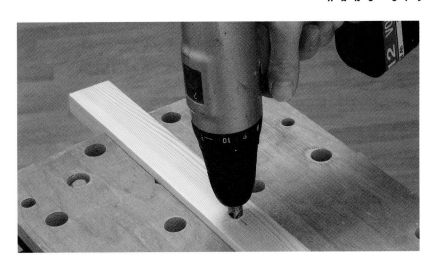

STEP 1 Cut the lumber lengths to fit. Mark the positions for the fixings (one screw per yard/meter of rail). Drill out the holes and mark the positions on the wall roughly 5ft/1.5m from the floor. Drill and anchor the holes.

STEP 2 Mark out the positions for the pegs along the rail. They should not be too close together; consider the room's proportions and allow a spacing of 12in–20in/300mm–500mm. Fit the spade bit to the drill and make the holes for the pegs (at an angle of 45°).

STEP 3 If using dowel, cut it into 4-in/100-mm lengths for the pegs. Smooth the exposed ends to a neat rounded finish and rub the sides of the "sinking" ends on the sandpaper to slim them slightly so that they fit snugly into the drilled holes.

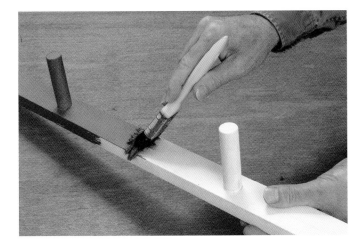

STEP 4 Squeeze wood glue into the holes and coat the sinking ends of the pegs. Tap them in position, then wipe away any excess glue. Leave to set. Paint the pegs and the rail in your chosen color.

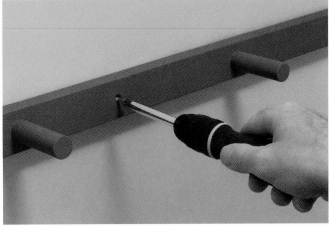

STEP 5 Finally, screw the peg rail onto the wall, then cover the screwheads with wood filler and touch up with paint once it has dried.

YOU WILL NEED:
• STEEL OR CHROME
  ROD WITH HOOKS (OR
  TWO CHROME TOWEL
  RAIL HOLDERS AND A
  LENGTH OF RAIL)
• STRAIGHT EDGE
  WITH A BUILT-IN
  SPIRIT LEVEL
• PAINTER'S TAPE IF
  THE WALL IS TILED
• DRILL
• CORRECT SIZE
  MASONRY DRILL
  BIT FOR THE SCREWS
  (E.G. SCREW SIZE
  No. 6, BIT SIZE No. 6)
• WALL ANCHORS

PROJECT TWO

Fitting a chrome utensil rod to the wall

The first thing you need to discover is what your wall is made of. The usual suspects are painted or tiled brick or wallboard, and they require different wall fixings. There is also a knack to drilling holes in tiles successfully. Use a small strip of painter's tape that has to be placed on the tile before you mark the screw position. The tape stops the drill bit from skidding off as it spins. Whether you buy a ready-made rod or make one yourself by customizing a chrome towel rod, the actual task of fitting it to the wall will be the same.

Chrome utensil rods can be bought ready-made, or you can make them by customizing a chrome towel rod. When you are deciding which height to fit it, hang the longest utensil from the rod to make sure it's high enough.

HOW TO DO IT

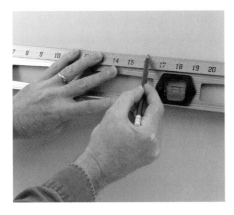

STEP 1 Decide where you would like the rod on the wall and mark the position in pencil. Hold up the rod to the wall with the spirit level. Make certain that the rod is level, then accurately mark the positions for the screws.

STEP 2 Drill the holes for the wall anchors. Hold the drill at a right angle to the wall and apply firm pressure as you drill.

TIPS

• Chrome rods can be clamped to a workbench or a table edge, and cut down to size with a hacksaw.

• Wooden doweling rods can be used with chrome towel rod fittings to give a softer look. They are especially suitable if you have wooden floors or cupboard doors.

• Buy butcher-style hooks, without sharp points, from kitchenware stores.

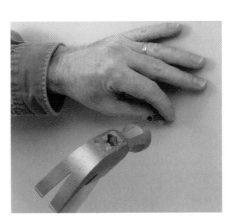

STEP 3 Push the anchors into the holes, tapping them lightly with a hammer if necessary. They should fit snugly and stay in place. If the hole is too big you may need to go up a size with both wall anchors and screws.

STEP 4 Screw in the top screw on each side to support the rod as you tighten the other screws.

PROJECT THREE

Fitting a rod below a floating shelf

Shelves with internal brackets give the kitchen a contemporary edge, and by fitting steel rods for cups below the shelf you can double its usefulness. If you are displaying glasses, cups, or mugs in this way invest in a brand new matching set so that you can enjoy looking at them. Buy the shelves from a hardware store: they will come with full fitting instructions and the fixings needed to complete the job. The design of the steel rod is best kept simple—as a rule the cheaper they are, the more elaborate —so shop around for a rail that pleases the eye. Some of them can be bought with hooks, if not, buy blunt "S" hooks rather than butcher's hooks, which have lethal points.

Open shelves fitted with steel rods provide useful storage space without blocking out areas of the galley kitchen. Matching sets of crockery are preferable to odd sets, if you are putting them on display in a modern kitchen.

HOW TO DO IT

STEP 1 Use the backsaw and miter block to cut the supports for the rod.

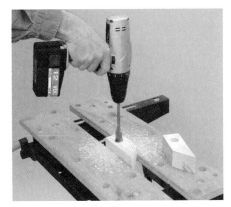

STEP 2 Use the ⅞-in/22-mm spade bit to drill holes in the supports to take the rod. Drill to ⅝-in/15-mm depth.

STEP 3 Drill a 4-mm clearance hole through the shelf. Countersink for the screw head. Drill a pilot hole into the bracket for the screw. Repeat for the other support.

STEP 4 Fit the pipe into the hole of the fixed support, and then fit the second support at the other end of the shelf. Screw this in position from above.

YOU WILL NEED:

• 3 x 1-IN/75 x 25-MM
PAR SOFTWOOD TO
FIT AROUND THE
ROOM (MEASURE THE
LENGTH REQUIRED)

• SHELF (THE SAME
AMOUNT OF PAR
SOFTWOOD AGAIN)

• SUPPORT BRACKETS
FOR SHELF TO
MATCH 3IN/75MM
DEPTH OF SHELF

• PEGS (EITHER BUY
TURNED PEGS OR
MAKE THEM FROM
A LENGTH OF DOWEL.
DECIDE HOW MANY
YOU NEED FOR NOW,
MORE CAN ALWAYS
BE ADDED LATER)

• STRAIGHT EDGE WITH
BUILT-IN SPIRIT LEVEL

• PENCIL

• DRILL

• $5/16$-IN/8-MM BIT FOR
CLEARANCE HOLES

• $1/4$-IN/6-MM BIT
FOR WALL FIXINGS

• $1/8$-IN/2-MM BIT
FOR PILOT HOLES

• SPADE BIT FOR PEGS

• $1/4$-IN/6-MM WALL
ANCHORS SUITABLE
FOR YOUR WALL

A row of pegs can make clearing up fun. Hang a row of brightly colored bags on the pegs to put small toys like bricks, cars, or marbles in, or hang the toys directly on the pegs themselves. The shelf above offers even more storage space.

PROJECT FOUR
Fitting a peg rail and shelf

This could be a continuation of some tongue-and-groove paneling, which always looks brilliant in kid's playrooms, or a project on its own. If you decide against paneling, you may not want to fit the peg rail and shelf on more than one wall. The instructions allow for this, and explain the order and technique rather than giving exact measurements so it can be adapted.

HOW TO DO IT

STEP 1 Cut the peg rail plank to fit the wall lengths, mitering the ends for a neat fit in the corners and at any joints. Check and mark the rail position on the wall with a spirit level.

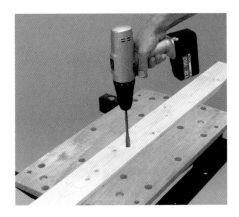

STEP 2 Use the spade bit to drill holes for the pegs and then apply wood glue to their ends before pushing them firmly into the rail. If the pegs are to be painted different colors, it may be easier to do this before you fit them.

STEP 3 Drill clearance holes in the planks then mark, drill, and anchor to the wall or wall batten, and screw the peg rail in place.

STEP 4 Screw the shelf to the peg rail or through into the wall batten. Prime and paint.

PROJECT FIVE

Pegboard or softboard wall covering

YOU WILL NEED:
- PEGBOARD OR SOFTBOARD
- MOLDING FOR FRAME SURROUND
- MITER SAW TO CUT FRAME CORNERS
- DRILL, WALL ANCHORS, AND SCREWS TO FIX THE FRAME TO THE WALL
- PANEL ADHESIVE FOR SOFTBOARD

(FOR THE PEGBOARD)
- 1 x 1-IN/25 x 25-MM CLEATS FOR PEGBOARD
- HARDBOARD PINS
- SMALL HAMMER AND PEGS

Pegboard is perforated hardboard that can be used to cover sections or complete walls. It not only looks good, retro, and funky, but provides a really useful storage surface. The holes are used for hooks and pegs for hanging containers, small boxes, speakers, and other gizmos. An alternative, useful, and inexpensive material is softboard, which is usually used as a liner for school corridor walls. It is very lightweight, and can be stuck onto the wall with panel adhesive and then painted for use as a notice board.

Softboard makes an ideal noticeboard because it is lightweight, so it can be stuck on the wall with panel adhesive and painted a favorite color. A few pin-ups and other teenage collectables will do the rest.

HOW TO DO IT

STEP 1 For the softboard, hold it against the wall and mark the position of the corners. Apply panel adhesive to the back of the softboard, and stick it onto the wall. For the pegboard, plug and screw the cleats to the wall with hardboard pins.

STEP 2 Hold the molding up to the wall and mark the position of the miters. Cut the frame corners with the mitering saw. Drill clearance holes in three places along the length of each side. Mark the screw positions on the walls, and then drill and anchor. Apply panel adhesive to the back of the moldings and screw them to the wall.

STEP 3 Paint the softboard or pegboard to blend in or contrast with the wall color. Two coats may be necessary for the softboard, because it is highly absorbent.

Cabinet Makeovers

Updating your existing furniture is the name of the
decorating game these days, and kitchen cabinets are often the first to
get the makeover treatment, especially if they are dull and made of melamine!
This chapter shows you how easy it is to replace the existing doors on your old
units with new and funky ones, chicken-wire panels, or even how to ditch the
doors altogether and use wicker baskets instead. But you don't even have to
go that far—a coat of primer and bright paint makes for a quick and easy
transformation, or you could experiment with different waxes,
washes, or other textured finishes.

YOU WILL NEED:

- READYMADE DOOR OR A SHEET OF BEECH-FACED MDF
- SANDPAPER (IF YOU ARE MAKING A NEW DOOR)
- STEEL DOOR HANDLE WITH SCREWS
- NEW SPRING-LOADED HINGES (ONLY IF THE OLD ONES NEED REPLACING)
- SCREWDRIVER
- SCREWS
- ⅛-IN/2-MM DRILL BIT FOR PILOT HOLES
- DRILL
- SPECIAL 1⅜-IN/ 35-MM SPADE BIT (IF YOU ARE RE-FITTING CONCEALED HINGES)
- PENCIL
- SPIRIT LEVEL

PROJECT ONE

Replacing existing doors

A change of doors on the kitchen units is one of the quickest ways to create a new look. Fitted kitchen units are made to a standard size and, although the hinges look quite complex, they are not difficult to fit. Ready-made hardwood doors are widely available, and it makes sense to use them if the style is right.

The other option is to make them yourself using beech-faced MDF. The MDF backing makes it easy to work with, and the beech facing has all the beauty of the natural grain. You can buy it from most reputable lumber merchants in sheets measuring 48 x 96in/1.2 x 2.4m in a standard ¾-in/19-mm thickness.

Replacing kitchen unit doors is one of the quickest ways to create a new look. Because fitted kitchen units are made to a standard size, you can buy them ready-made. Add chrome handles to complete the look.

HOW TO DO IT

STEP 1 Support the door as you unscrew the hinges to remove it. If the screws are in a good condition, save them to re-use in the new door.

STEP 2 If you are making a new door, then use the old one as a template to draw around. Check the right angles and the measurements, and then cut out the new door with a handsaw and sandpaper the edges.

STEP 3 Mark the positions for the hinge fittings, and drill out the recess with the spade bit.

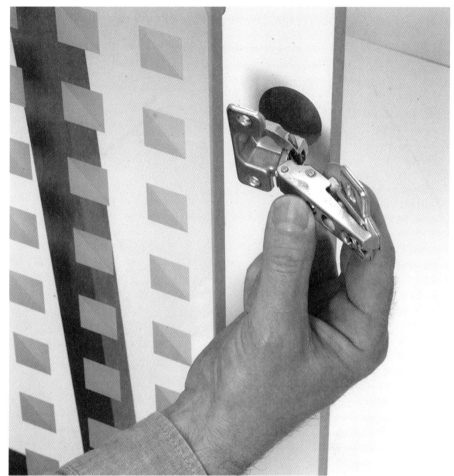

STEP 4 Hold the door in position with the hinge mechanism fitted into the recess, and mark the screw positions. Drill small pilot holes.

STEP 5 Screw the hinges to the doors. The fit of the door can be adjusted using the two screws on the hinge inside the cupboard. Loosen the screws, move the door slightly, and re-tighten them. Repeat this sequence until the fit is perfect.

STEP 6 Measure the positions for the screws or bolts accurately. The handles on all the doors must be perfectly aligned, so double-check and use a spirit level. Drill holes for the screws or bolts, and fit the handles.

YOU WILL NEED:
- $^{3}/_{8}$-IN/9-MM MDF
- FINE-GRADE
  SANDPAPER
- FACE MASK
- JIGSAW
- $^{1}/_{8}$-IN/2-MM DRILL BIT
  FOR PILOT HOLES
- $^{5}/_{16}$-IN/8-MM DRILL BIT
- ALL-SURFACE PRIMER
- PAINT (SEMIGLOSS OR
  EGGSHELL FINISH)
- SMALL FOAM PAINT
  ROLLER AND TRAY
- $^{1}/_{2}$-IN/12-MM CHICKEN
  WIRE (OR NEAREST
  GAUGE TO THIS)
- WIRE CUTTERS
- SMALL HAMMER
- STAPLE GUN

PROJECT TWO

Replacing cupboard doors with chicken wire, framed in MDF

This project is suitable for wall-mounted kitchen or base units. If you like the look you could use it throughout the kitchen, but remember that you can see through chicken wire and not everything in a cupboard makes a good display.

Begin by emptying the cupboard and unscrewing the door. Kitchen cupboard hinges tend to leave large holes which will need filling if you are changing the style. Clean the inside of the cupboard with a grease-cutting detergent and paint it a country color—pale moss green or slate blue, for instance. Melamine will need to be primed first, ideally with an all-surface primer. If you are lining the shelves, do it at this stage before the door is replaced.

Replacing existing cupboard doors with chicken wire suits the country-kitchen look because it puts more of your kitchen on show. It's a good idea to plan the contents of the cupboards before you decide to put them on display.

HOW TO DO IT

STEP 1 Place your outgoing door on top of the MDF. Use it as as a template, drawing the outline onto the MDF. Clamp the MDF on a workbench and wear the mask as you cut it to size, and sand the edges lightly.

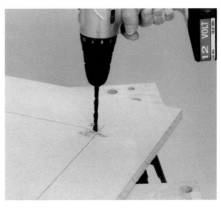

STEP 2 Draw the cut-out shape onto the MDF. Drill a hole in one corner of the shape, using an ⅝-in/8-mm drill bit.

STEP 3 Clamp the MDF to the workbench and jigsaw out the inside shape. Keep the jigsaw's foot in touch with the surface of the MDF, and move with the saw.

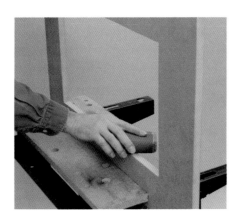

STEP 4 Use sandpaper to smooth the edge on the inside and outside. Always wear a mask when sanding MDF to prevent you breathing in the fine particles which contain chemicals that are best avoided!

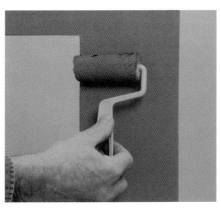

STEP 5 Give the door two coats of primer, following the drying times as directed on the can. Use a foam roller to apply the paint because it will give a better finish than a brush, and painting takes half the time. Apply the top coat in the same way.

STEP 6 Cut the chicken wire to the size of the cut-out shape allowing an extra 1in/25mm all around the edge. Turn over a seam of ⅜in/10mm and flatten it with a hammer. Lay the MDF face down with the chicken wire in position at the back. Staple the panel at the four cardinal points first, then add more staples in between until it is perfectly secure. Re-hang the door.

TIP
• Even with a folded seam, chicken wire has sharp pointy edges. As long as the shelves in the cupboard are set back from the door, it is a good idea to cover up these edges with a simple wooden molding.
• Measure the lengths required, then miter the corners and use brads to secure them.

YOU WILL NEED:
- SCREWDRIVER
- WOOD FILLER
- MOLDING
- MITER SAW (OR BACKSAW AND MITER BLOCK)
- MEDIUM-GRADE SANDPAPER
- CONTACT ADHESIVE
- MOLDING PINS
- CENTER PUNCH
- SMALL HAMMER
- ALL-PURPOSE PRIMER
- PAINT (IN A SUITABLE COUNTRY COLOR)
- SMALL FOAM PAINT ROLLER AND TRAY
- WILLOW BASKETS

PROJECT THREE

Removing cupboard doors and adding willow baskets

Any base unit or kitchen cupboard can be given a real country look by removing the doors, and using willow baskets on the shelves as pull-out drawers. In fact, it may require a leap of the imagination to convert a standard beige melamine cupboard into something beautiful, but it can be done! All you need do is whip off the doors, fill the holes, and pop in the baskets, but a few trimmings will make all the difference.

A melamine cupboard can be painted after suitable priming, and the facing edges of the cupboard can be covered with a wooden molding. They come in a range of styles, from twisted rope and oak leaves to simple half-moon and square edge. The inside of the cupboard will look good painted in a contrasting color to the outside, and there is also the option of adding a curtain on a simple net wire. Plaid or even linen tea towel curtains look a million times better than old melamine, and they can be tied back attractively to reveal the baskets inside.

Willow baskets as sliding, pull-out shelves transform standard melamine cupboards. Paint the insides and outsides of the cupboard first, and add wooden molding to the facing edges.

HOW TO DO IT

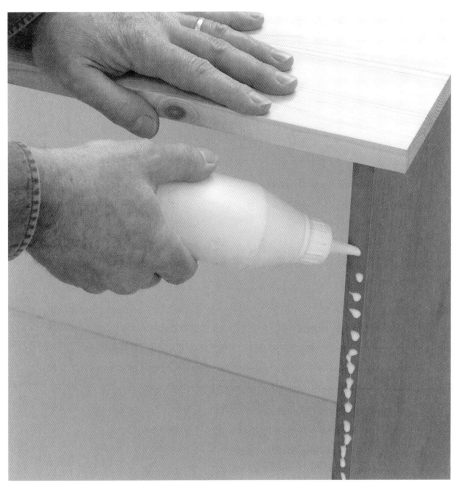

STEP 1 Unscrew the existing doors and remove the fittings. Fill the holes with wood filler so that the filler stands slightly proud of the surface. Once it has dried, sand the filler level.

STEP 2 Measure the frame then cut the molding to fit, mitering the corners. Apply contact adhesive to the frame.

BASKET HANDLE IDEAS
You can use any of the following...
- Cardboard parcel labels tied on with string
- Checked ribbons
- Stitched tubes of fabric
- Threaded beads or buttons on twists of wire
- Rope loops
- Buckled leather straps

STEP 3 Stick the molding down and then add a few pins along each length. Tap the pinheads into the molding with a center punch, fill the holes, and sand smooth.

STEP 4 Prime the cupboard and then paint it inside and out. If you are using two different colors, paint the inside of the cupboard first and allow it to dry before painting the area where the colors meet.

STEP 5 Buy willow baskets to fill the space widthwise, leaving just enough room for them to slide easily in and out. Many baskets have handles attached, but if not there are plenty of ways to make your own.

YOU WILL NEED:
- LUMBER (SEE LUMBER REQUIREMENTS, RIGHT) PLUS SMALL SCRAP OF WOOD TO MAKE A CATCH
- 4 HINGES
- 1 IRON BOLT
- SMALL BRADS
- WOOD GLUE
- HAMMER
- SANDPAPER
- HANDSAW
- SCREWDRIVER
- SMALL SCREWS
- AWL
- 6 CUP HOOKS
- 2 MIRROR FIXINGS
- RUST RED PAINT
- PAINT BRUSH
- WALL FIXINGS

PROJECT FOUR

A small shuttered wall cupboard

This shallow cabinet looks like a wooden shuttered window you would find in a farmhouse. On the wall in an entrance hall it creates the illusion of a window, when it is actually a key cabinet. Recycled lumber gives the most rustic effect—or use part of a small louvered door.

The idea is to make a box with a decorative lid to hang on the wall. For the backing plate, use lumber thick enough to allow for hooks to be screwed in. The traditional colors used for shuttered windows are red-brown or blue-green, both of which soon fade and mellow in the bright sunshine.

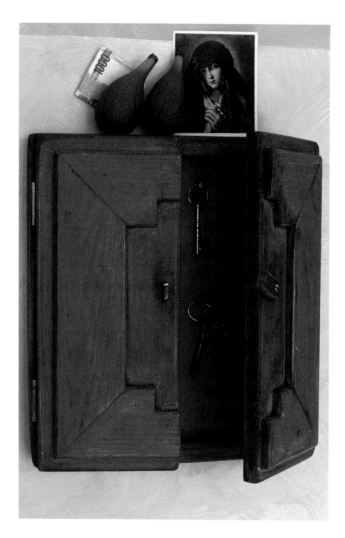

This Italian-style key cupboard will look great painted in muted Mediterranean colors with dappled sunlight falling across it.

TEMPLATE

Draw a template based on these designs. The cupboard made here is 11½ x 13 x 1in/290 x 330 x 25mm, but adapt your template to the size you require.

LUMBER REQUIREMENTS

back: 11½ x 13in/290 x 330mm;

sides: 2 x 1 x 1in/25 x 25mm, measuring 11½in/290mm;

top/bottom: 2 x 1 x 1in/25 x 25mm, measuring 11¼in/285mm

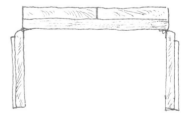

doors: 5½ x 12½in/140 x 325mm

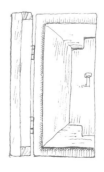

paneling:
2¼ x 11½in long mitered/
70 x 290mm
2¼ x 4⅞in long mitered/
70 x 125mm

HOW TO DO IT

This idea can be adapted to suit your needs or the lumber you have available. The cupboard is simply glued and pinned together.

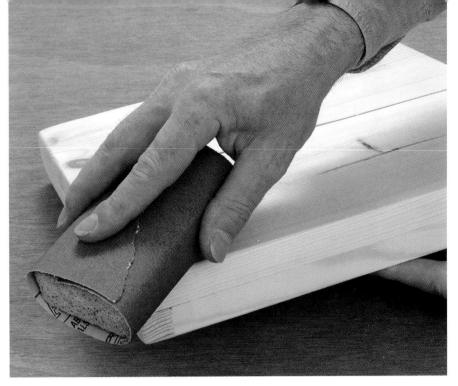

STEP 1 Cut all the pieces to size (see lumber requirements, opposite). Sand as necessary.

STEP 2 Make up the shallow box with simple butt joints, using wood glue and brads to secure the sides and fix them to the back.

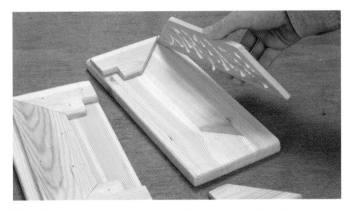

STEP 3 Make up the two front doors, adding extra panels and cross bars to give the shutter style (if required).

STEP 4 Attach the doors to the box base using two hinges for each door.

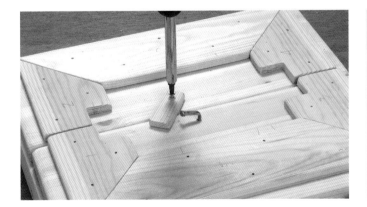

STEP 5 Fix the iron bolt onto the front to join the doors in the middle.

STEP 6 Apply two coats of paint. When the cupboard is dry, screw six hooks (or more) into the back of it, then fit the mirror fixings onto the back and fix the cupboard onto the wall.

YOU WILL NEED:

• SILICONE-CARBIDE
  SANDPAPER

• ALL-SURFACE PRIMER

• SMALL FOAM ROLLER
  WITH TRAY

• METHYLATED
  ALCOHOL (FOR
  CLEANING)

• SEMIGLOSS PAINT
  PAINT IN PALE GREEN
  (MAIN COLOR)

• STENCIL MATERIAL
  (CARD OR PLASTIC)

• SNAP-BLADE KNIFE

• TRACING PAPER
  (OR PHOTOCOPIES
  OF PATTERNS)

• TEST POT OF BRIGHT
  RED (BACK-
  GROUND COLOR)

• TEST POT OF BLACK
  (FOR THE PATTERN)

PROJECT FIVE

Painting the kitchen units

The idea that melamine kitchen units can be painted is actually quite new. This has a lot to do with TV makeover programs and the popularity of home-style magazines. Once the makeover idea took off, people started experimenting, trying different products and discovering new uses for old materials. The problem with a shiny surface like melamine is that, without the right primer, the paint has nothing to key into and is easily scratched. The trick is to scratch the surface with a silicone-carbide sandpaper, then apply one or two coats of a shellac-based primer. It gives good coverage, is very strong, and leaves an ultra-mat surface.

Go creative on your kitchen units! Melamine kitchen units can be painted, so long as they are prepared beforehand, using sandpaper to scratch the surface and primer to give an ultra-mat surface.

HOW TO DO IT

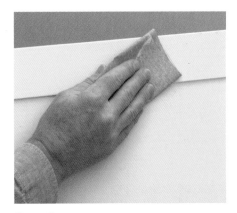

STEP 1 Clean the doors with a grease-cutting detergent or abrasive powder. Rub them down with silicone-carbide sandpaper to remove the shine from the surface.

STEP 2 Apply the primer with the roller and leave to dry (repeat if necessary). Apply the main color (repeat if necessary).

STEP 3 Enlarge the two stencil patterns and transfer them onto stencil card or plastic. Cut them out with a snap-blade knife. Paint the background shapes first in the light color. Use the second stencil to apply the pattern inside the shapes, and then apply two coats of clear enamel varnish.

Enlarge the stencils and transfer them onto plastic or stencil paper. The guides to the left will help you position the two main stencils together on your kitchen unit door.

PROJECT SIX

Revamping a wooden cupboard

Several different finishes—paint, colorwash, stain, varnish, and wax—are used, together with replacement glass and simple brass furniture, to give this well-made but badly neglected cupboard and drawer combination unit a new lease of life.

HOW TO DO IT

STEP 1 The old multilayered paint finish is removed using a scraper to take off blistered paint after applying water-washable paint stripper. Remember to wear gloves!

STEP 2 When all the paint is removed, steel wool dipped in sugar soap is used to clean the surface thoroughly. Always rub in the direction of the woodgrain.

STEP 3 The door is removed and cleaned, and old glass, molding, and putty discarded. A coat of white latex is "distressed."

STEP 4 The inside of the cupboard needs to reflect a warm, friendly glow; orange latex paint from a sample pot is ideal.

STEP 5 Diluted woodwash (available in small cans) is painted onto the base and top of the unit. Turquoise was the chosen color here.

STEP 6 The multi-finish theme continues—diluted ultramarine water-based dye is brushed into the side grain, avoiding the front edge.

STEP 7 The front will remain as bare wood, cleaned up with 240 grit aluminum oxide wrapped around a sanding block.

STEP 8 The waxed drawer is tested to ensure it slides well. Blue and white waxes have been applied and polished.

STEP 9 New brass drawer and cabinet door furniture is fitted to replace the old plastic knobs. Small hands and a stubby screwdriver are needed to gain access to the inside of the drawers.

Hidden Assets

Not everything in your home is worthy of being put
on show, and sometimes it's necessary to hide or disguise certain vital
yet unattractive items. Television and video equipment is a good example:
it does tend to clutter up the living room, so why not hide it behind an
attractively covered screen? Garish videos can also be stowed away in a neat
drawer which is painted to match the baseboard exactly. Kitchen equipment
can also be discreetly hidden, and both a toaster and a food mixer can wear
smart padded covers. Out-of-season clothes—great wardrobe space
devourers—get the same treatment and can be tucked away under
the bed in soft, collapsible cases.

YOU WILL NEED:
- 1 x 2IN/25 x 50MM LUMBER FOR THE FRAMES
- TO MAKE A TWO-PANEL SCREEN OVERALL SIZE 60 x 30IN/1500MM HIGH x 750MM WIDE, YOU WILL NEED 2 x 1IN/ 50 x 25MM LUMBER FOR THE FRAMES CUT INTO 4 x 60IN/1500MM AND 4 x 14¹/₂IN/375MM
- 4 SMALL DOOR KNOBS FOR FEET
- MITERING SAW (OR BACKSAW AND MITERING BLOCK)
- TAPE MEASURE
- PENCIL
- WOOD GLUE
- THIN BRADS
- SMALL HAMMER
- 3 TWO-WAY HINGES AND SCREWS TO FIT
- BRADAWL
- SCREWDRIVER
- SCREWS
- STAPLE GUN
- WOOD PRIMER AND UNDERCOAT
- PAINT—SEMIGLOSS OR EGGSHELL FOR A MAT FINISH
- SMALL ENAMEL ROLLER AND TRAY

TO FILL EACH FRAME YOU NEED:
- PANEL OF HEAVY UPHOLSTERY FABRIC, TAPESTRY OR IKAT (TIE-DYED) STYLE
- BRAID FOR TRIMMING
- FABRIC ADHESIVE

A folding screen is a portable and decorative way of hiding modern equipment such as computers, televisions, and video recorders.

PROJECT ONE

Making a two-panel screen to hide modern equipment

All your efforts to recreate the atmosphere of a traditional sitting room can be ruined by televisions, computers, and video recorders. They attract the eye even when they are not switched on. Furniture stores now stock antique reproduction cabinets to conceal high-tech appliances, but they do tend to be expensive and look cheap. If you watch a lot of television it isn't practical to hide it in a cupboard, but you could take it off its stand and put it on something more in keeping with the room's style, such as a tin trunk or a wooden chest. If the room has an alcove, push the equipment back into it, and fit a wide shelf at least 12in/300mm above it. A blind or curtain can be fitted along the shelf edge to conceal everything when not in use. A folding screen is an even easier solution, and it also offers more decorative possibilities.

HOW TO DO IT

STEP 1 Apply wood glue to the joining edges and assemble the frames. Screw to fasten. Paint the frames and the molding with a primer, an undercoat, and the final top coat.

STEP 2 Lay the frame over the fabric and cut, leaving at least 1½in/38mm as an overlap.

STEP 3 Stretch the fabric taut and staple it to the back of the frame. Place the first four staples halfway along each side, then staple the corners and several points in between.

STEP 4 Measure the lengths of braid needed to cover the edges. Miter the corners then apply fabric adhesive to the back edges.

STEP 5 Lay the two screen panels flat, butted up together, and place hinges 4in/100mm from the top and bottom, with one in the middle. Use the bradawl to make small pilot holes for the screws.

STEP 6 Small round feet can be added using brass or wooden cupboard door knobs screwed into the base of the frames.

VARIATIONS
• Fit the sheets of woven cane in the same way as the fabric.
• Use small screws to secure the fretwork panels to the frames. You will need to drill clearance holes along the panel edges, and use a bradawl to make pilot holes for the screws. Paint the panels to match or contrast with the frames.

YOU WILL NEED:

- 8 SMALL CASTORS
- LENGTH OF BASEBOARD TO MATCH THE EXISTING ONE (IF IT CAN'T BE RE-USED)
- PANEL ADHESIVE
- 2 x 1-IN/50 x 25-MM BATTEN
- ½-IN/12-MM MDF SHEET FOR SHELF
- ¼-IN/6-MM MDF FOR DRAWER BASE
- ¼-IN/6-MM MDF FOR 4 DRAWER SIDES
- HANDSAW
- THIN BRADS
- SMALL HAMMER
- PAINT AND A BRUSH
- SPIRIT LEVEL
- DRILL
- MASONRY BIT
- WALL ANCHORS
- ³⁄₁₆-IN/4-MM DRILL BIT FOR WOOD
- ⅛-IN/2-MM DRILL BIT FOR PILOT HOLES
- SCREWS

PROJECT TWO
Disguised storage

If you really want to disguise something the trick is to make it look the same as everything around it. This project does this by building a boxed-in shelf with a drawer at floor level, and using a baseboard front to disguise it so well that it could almost be used as a safe. This is also a way to make the most of an alcove by building the shelf wide enough for the TV. If the alcove is not deep enough it will need to be built out at the front, but the basic idea remains the same.

This drawer on castors has been built as part of a low, boxed-in shelf, and disguised with a baseboard front to blend in with the edges around it.

HOW TO DO IT

STEP 1 Measure the depth of the alcove. If it needs extending, take this into account and cut out 2 side pieces of 2 x 1in/25 x 50mm to support the shelf. If the shelf height is 19³⁄₄in/500mm the sides will need to be 19¹⁄₄in/488mm. Drill and screw to the wall and then check the level.

STEP 2 Cut the shelf to fit the alcove. Cut a U-shape cable hole on the back edge. Apply a long bead of adhesive to the top edges of the sides and place the shelf on top. Use a hammer to drive in some thin brads to hold the shelf securely. If the alcove is wide, add a supporting leg to the middle.

STEP 3 Make up the two drawers: cut the base of each drawer to fit snugly inside the alcove allowing just enough clearance for it to slide in and out without catching.

STEP 4 Cut drawer sides to match the depth of the shelf, and a front and back to be butted into them.

STEP 5 Fit four castors to the base of each drawer.

STEP 6 Cut the baseboard to fit onto the drawer front (and box sides if the shelf has been built out beyond the alcove). Stick the baseboard onto the drawer front (and box sides if built out) with panel adhesive. Do this so that the baseboard skims the floor, hiding the castors. Paint the sides and front of the drawers to match the walls and the new baseboard to match the old baseboard.

YOU WILL NEED:
- STRIPED TICKING
  FABRIC
- 2 x 3FT 3-IN/
  1000-MM ZIPPERS
- PINS
- SEWING MACHINE
- ZIPPER FOOT
- NEEDLE AND THREAD
- PINKING SHEARS
- STEAM IRON
- SCISSORS

PROJECT THREE
Underbed case

The empty space under the bed is often neglected as a storage area, yet it is ideal for storing spare bed-linen and out-of-season clothing. The items need to be concealed inside containers to protect them from dust: a slim fabric case with a deep gusset can hold many items. You will need two 3ft 3-in/ 1000-mm zippers.

Store out-of-season clothes and bed-linen in a smart, striped, underbed case. This can be stored away unobtrusively.

HOW TO DO IT

STEP 1 Cut a strip of fabric for the base gusset 6ft 6in x 5¾in/2000 x 145mm, and a strip of fabric for the lid gusset 6ft 6in x 2¼in/2000 x 56mm. Press ⅝in/15mm under on one long edge of both pieces, and mark the centers of the pressed edges with a pin.

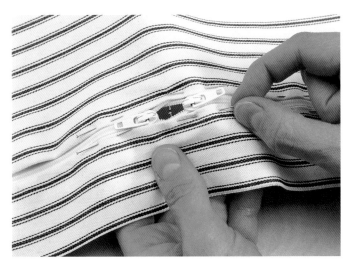

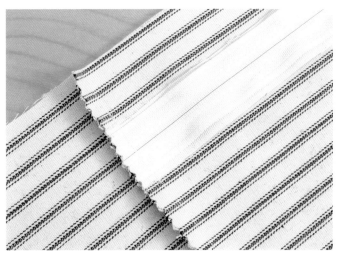

STEP 2 Pin two 3ft 3-in/1000-mm zippers under the pressed edges, with the top ends ⅜in/10mm each side of the center pins, positioning the pressed edges against the zipper teeth. Zippers cut from a continuous length will be unfinished at the top, so open the top of the zippers a little and pin the top teeth under the pressed edges so that the zippers do not slip off before stitching. Using a zipper foot, stitch close to each side of the zipper.

STEP 3 Cut a strip of fabric for the back gusset 3ft 6¼in x 7in/1080 x 178mm. With the right sides facing, stitch the ends of the zippered gussets to the ends of the back gusset, taking a ⅜-in/10-mm seam allowance, and starting and finishing the seams ⅜in/10mm from the long edges. Neaten the seams with pinking shears or a zigzag stitch. Press toward the back gusset.

STEP 4 Partly unzip the zippers to turn right side out. Cut two rectangles of fabric 3ft 6¼in x 18½in/1080 x 472mm for the lid and base. Open out the back seam at the top of the lid gusset. With the right sides facing, pin the back gusset to one long edge of the lid, then continue pinning the lid gusset to the lid. Snip the gusset at the front corners of the lid so the fabric lies smoothly. Stitch in place, taking a ⅜-in/10-mm seam allowance, and pivoting the seam at the corners. Stitch the base gusset to the base in the same way. Neaten the seams with pinking shears or a zigzag stitch. Turn right side out.

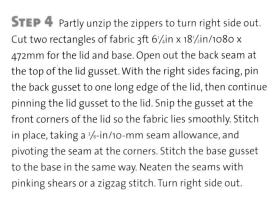

YOU WILL NEED:
- FABRIC OF
  YOUR CHOICE
- PATTERN PAPER
- LINING
- BATTING
- PINS
- NEEDLE AND THREAD
- SEWING MACHINE
- TAPE MEASURE
- PENCIL
- AIR-ERASABLE PEN
- CONTRASTING FABRIC
  FOR BINDING
- SCISSORS

PROJECT FOUR

Toaster and food mixer covers

Coordinate your kitchen appliances with a set of matching covers made from light-to-mediumweight fabrics. Here, linen-look fabrics in contemporary designs have a contrasting, striped fabric for the lining and binding.

Because toasters and food mixers vary in size, you will need to make your own paper pattern. Measure the height and depth of the machine, and add 1¼in/32mm to the measurements. Draw a square or rectangle on paper to these measurements for the end panel. Round off the

top corners by drawing around an upturned glass. Cut out the pattern and check it against the end of the toaster or mixer; it should be at least ⅜in/10mm larger on all sides. Draw the grain line parallel with the side edges.

For the front and back panels, use a tape measure to measure around the sides and top of the end panel pattern, from one corner of the base edge to the other corner of the base edge. Measure the length of the toaster, and add 1¼in/32mm to this measurement.

A set of matching appliance covers can look very stylish, especially if you choose fabric that blends in with your color scheme.

HOW TO DO IT

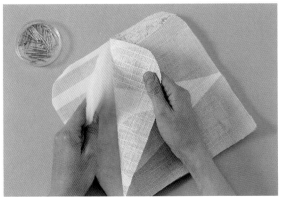

STEP 1 Use the pattern to cut two end panels from the fabric, lining, and 2oz/56g batting. Cut one rectangle each of the fabric, lining, and batting to the front and back panel measurements. Sandwich the batting between the fabric and lining, with the right sides facing outward. Baste the layers together along the outer edges.

STEP 2 Set the sewing machine to a slightly longer stitch length than usual. Starting at the center of the upper edges, stitch along the length of the panels in random, wavy lines about 2³/₄in/70mm apart. (Draw guidelines with an air-erasable pen first if you prefer.)

STEP 3 With the wrong sides facing, pin and baste each end piece to the long edges of the front and back panel, taking a ³/₈-in/10-mm seam allowance.

STEP 4 Cut two 3¹/₄in/83mm-wide bias strips of contrast fabric the length of the front and back panel, to bind the end seams. Press the bindings lengthwise in half. The binding is applied double: pin each binding to the basted seam with the right sides of the binding, and front and back panel facing. Stitch, taking a ³/₈-in/10-mm seam allowance. Turn the pressed edges over the raw edges and slipstitch along the seam on the end panels.

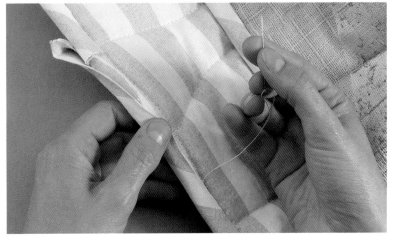

STEP 5 Cut an 3¹/₄in/83mm-wide bias strip of contrast fabric the length of the lower edge of the cover plus 1in/25mm. Press the binding lengthwise in half. Pin the binding to the lower edge with the right sides facing. Stitch, taking a ³/₈-in/10-mm seam allowance. Turn the pressed edges over the raw edges and slipstitch along the seam inside the cover.

Office Solutions

If you are working from home, then it is vital that you have
a designated work area and that you are as organized as possible—
which means having plenty of places to put paper, pens, and pencils, and other
associated office clutter. Children and teenagers also benefit from having a
decent desk at which to study. Cheap desks are easy to get hold of, and can be
customized in the latest acceptable teenage style. Moveable storage is always
useful, and the unit on wheels is large enough for box files and paperwork,
yet small enough for floppy disks and pencils. A free-standing desktop unit
is also described which, in theory, you could move to
wherever you wanted to work.

YOU WILL NEED:
- 1 PLAIN AND VERY INEXPENSIVE DESK (SECONDHAND IS BEST)
- 1 LARGE CAN OF ALUMINUM PAINT, PLUS SMALL CANS OF OTHER COLORS (YOU WILL NEED TWO COLORS FOR EACH NUMBER STENCIL THAT YOU CHOOSE)
- STENCIL CARD
- PENCIL
- CRAFT KNIFE
- PAINTER'S TAPE
- SPRAYMOUNT

PROJECT ONE

Customizing a cheap computer desk in the hip-hop style

Everyone needs somewhere to work, but that doesn't mean it has to look boring and worthy. This project takes a really inexpensive, white-laminated, fiberboard desk and gives it street cred. The numerals could be exchanged for letters done in the same shadowed style, and whatever pattern you choose, remember it doesn't matter if it's slightly off-center or if the spray drifts a bit at the edges—it'll still look really good.

A basketball-style stencil has transformed this inexpensive, white-laminated fiberboard desk. Add stickers, labels, and logos to complete the look.

HOW TO DO IT

STEP 1 Take a photocopy from a favorite sports sweatshirt.

STEP 2 Enlarge the numerals to about 12in/300mm in length and transfer the patterns onto the stencil card. Cut out two stencils. One should just be the letter outline, the other should have stencil bridges added on letters such as Os and Rs to keep the shape intact.

STEP 3 Use a craft knife to cut out the stencils. Spray the back with Spraymount. One stencil is for the main motif, the other for the border.

STEP 4 Protect a well-ventilated area with lots of newspaper, and then roller or brush the aluminum paint onto the desk.

STEP 5 Attach the first stencil to the desk with painter's tape. Spray this with your first chosen color.

STEP 6 Spray through the second stencil in the second color to create the border. Repeat this as many times as you like on the top, the outsides and insides, and then add as many stickers, logos, and labels as you like.

YOU WILL NEED:

- A SHEET OF ¾-IN/
  19-MM MDF CUT
  AS FOLLOWS:
  BACK 24 x 35IN/
  62 x 89CM
  TOP SHELF 12 x 35IN/
  30 x 89CM
  BOTTOM SHELF 9¾ x
  12IN/25 x 30CM
  SMALL SIDE SHELVES
  6 x 6IN/15 x 15CM
  (2 PIECES)
  LEFT-HAND SIDE
  24⅜ x 26IN/
  62 x 66CM
  RIGHT-HAND SIDE
  24⅜ x 8IN/
  62 x 20CM
  LEFT UPRIGHTS 17⅝ x
  12IN/45 x 30CM
  (2 PIECES)
  RIGHT UPRIGHTS 17⅝ x
  6IN/45 x 15CM
  (2 PIECES)
- No. 6 1½-IN/38-MM
  SCREWS
- WOOD GLUE
- WORKBENCH
- JIGSAW
- TAPE MEASURE
- COMBINATION
  SQUARE
- CARPENTER'S PENCIL
- DRILL WITH PILOT,
  SCREW, AND
  COUNTERSINK BIT
  (USE SIZE No. 4
  SCREWSINK BIT
  FOR ALL THREE)
- LONG RULE
- SANDPAPER
- SPIRIT LEVEL

When this desktop
unit is put on a table
it creates an instant
work surface. It keeps
all your desktop
clutter in an
organized space,
which can be quickly
put away after use.

PROJECT TWO
Building a desktop unit

The work surface can be a table or simply a sheet of thick board supported on a pair of trestles, but what turns it into an efficient desk are the drawer units, shelves, and storage space. This project shows how to build a free-standing unit to sit on top of the work surface. It includes space for the computer monitor, storage for CD-ROMs and discs, two file compartments, a stationery tray compartment, and a book-ended shelf on the top.

HOW TO DO IT

STEP 1 Hold the uprights, dividers, and shelves against the back section and mark out their positions in pencil on the back.

STEP 2 Draw, cut, and sand the mitered corners on the two sides.

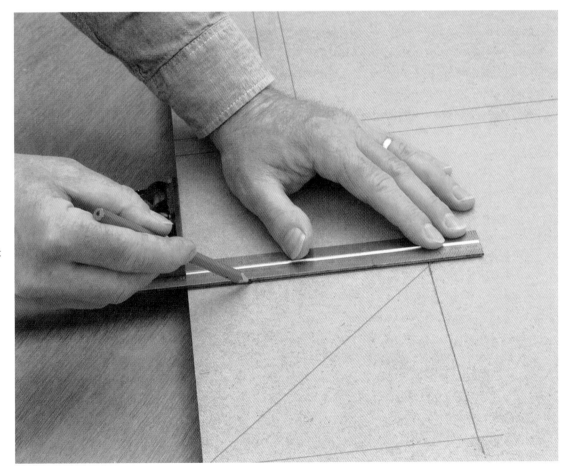

STEP 3 Measure and draw a 6-in/15-cm-square box at the bottom of the central section on the back piece. This will be cut out to serve as a channel for the computer cables.

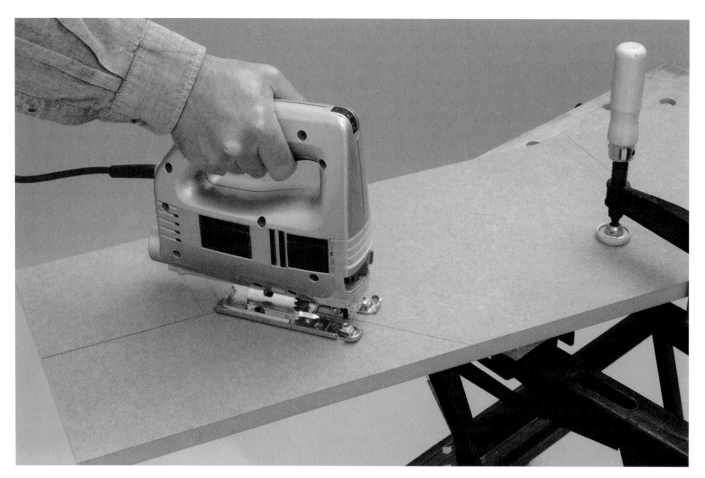

STEP 4 Use a jigsaw to cut out the cable box and the top shelf shape.

STEP 5 Drill clearance holes on the back section and countersink.

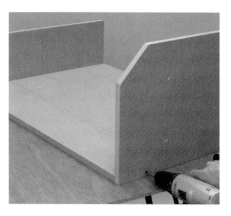

STEP 6 Fix the uprights to the back section.

STEP 7 Fix the sides to the two uprights. Fix the smaller shelves to the sides and back.

STEP 8 Fill the holes, sand, and paint in your chosen color.

Use this sketch to help you construct your desk. Remember to measure all the timber accurately and use a spirit level to ensure that everything is level.

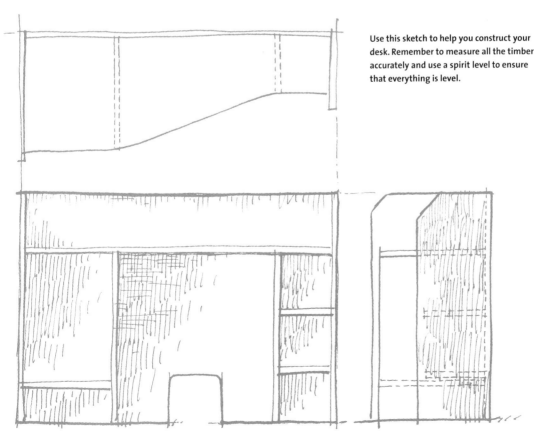

YOU WILL NEED:
- 1 SHEET OF
  3/4-IN/18-MM MDF
- LONG RULE
- TAPE MEASURE
- COMBINATION
  SQUARE
- PENCIL
- DRILL
- PILOT BIT AND
  COUNTERSINK BIT
- SCREWS
- STRAIGHT EDGE WITH
  BUILT-IN SPIRIT LEVEL
- 4 CASTORS
- WOOD GLUE
- SANDPAPER
- PAINT

PROJECT THREE

Storage

There is no getting away from storage. Whatever type of work you do, paperwork mounts up, records must be kept, and we all need somewhere to keep telephone books and reference material. This storage unit on castors will take care of books, files, and catalogs. The top is at desk height, so with a piece of MDF laid on top it provides an extra work surface.

This handy storage unit on castors keeps books, files, and catalogs accessible at the same time as neatly stored away. An optional top surface of MDF will make an additional work surface.

HOW TO DO IT

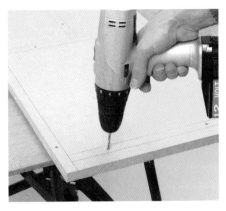

STEP 1 Cut the back of the unit from the sheet of MDF. It should be the height of your desk minus the height of the castors if you want to extend the desk area. Cut out all the shelves, dividers, and the top, sides, and bottom of the unit.

STEP 2 Draw the positions of the sides, top, and bottom, and all the partitions and shelves in pencil on the back. Use a length of MDF to do this so that you can see a flat plan of the unit on the back.

STEP 3 Drill clearance holes to fix all the pieces to the back of the unit. Hold each piece in position as you drill through the clearance holes to make pilot holes for the screws.

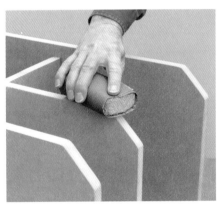

STEP 4 Assemble the outer frame first, applying wood glue to the joining edges before screwing them together through the back. Drill pilot, clearance, and countersink holes, then secure the corner joints by screwing them together. Fit all the partitions in place first, and then add the shelves. Drill, glue, and screw each one so that the whole unit stands firm.

STEP 5 Finally drill holes and fit the four castors onto the base of the unit.

STEP 6 Sand all the sharp edges smooth, then paint if required, or use it just as it is.

YOU WILL NEED:
- 1 SHEET OF 1-IN/ 25-MM MDF
- 4 DESK LEGS AND FITTINGS
- DRILL
- $^3/_{32}$-IN/2-MM DRILL BIT FOR PILOT HOLES
- JIGSAW
- PATTERN
- PENCIL
- 4 SQUARES OF WOOD TO MOUNT THE LEG FITTINGS ON
- $^3/_{16}$-IN/4-MM DRILL BIT FOR VERTICAL HOLES
- MDF PRIMER OR PVA
- PAINT OR STAIN
- SANDPAPER

PROJECT FOUR
Making a curved desk

You can make a very smart desk from one sheet of MDF and a pair of saw horses. Or you can buy the legs in sets of four, as shown in this project, which are then simply attached to the underside of the desk. This desk is ideal for someone whose desk is always piled high because it is shaped like a curve, so when you sit at it, everything is within arm's reach.

A simple curved desk made out of MDF is both stylish and functional. You can either buy a pair of saw horses or four, readymade legs.

HOW TO DO IT

STEP 1 Support the MDF between two saw horses. Draw the curve in pencil, either from the pattern or to your own plan. Cut out the curve with a jigsaw, and sand.

STEP 2 Support the desk leg in the work bench and drill a vertical hole for fitting, using the correct drill bit for your screws.

STEP 3 The leg fittings consist of two parts—one post with a screw fitting to fit into the leg and one to receive the post which fits under the table top.

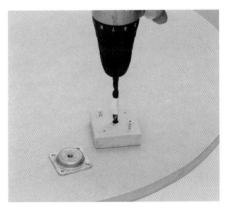

STEP 4 Screw the squares of timber to the underneath of the table, then mark the positions for the legs and all their screws. Drill pilot holes using a $^3/_{32}$-in/2-mm drill bit.

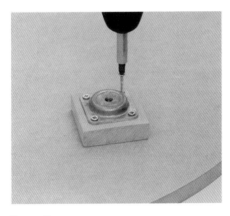

STEP 5 Screw the top receiving plate of the leg fitting into the timber boss.

STEP 6 Screw each leg into position. Lift the table and turn. Seal the surfaces with MDF primer or a 50:50 dilution of PVA and water. Paint, or stain and varnish the desk.

TIP
* These table legs are sold in packs in hardware stores, and always have instructions included with them. If you prefer, you could use saw horse legs, which can also be found in hardware stores.

Soft Options

Fabric storage systems are useful for more delicate items—
such as jewelry and special occasion outfits—and are flexible enough to
also store shoes, bed-linen, and children's toys. Drawstring bags make good
receptacles for cosmetics, such as cotton balls and cotton swabs, as well as
heavier items, while attractive lined baskets, which can be easily transported
from room to room, are useful for all that new-baby paraphernalia. An entire
closet front can even be constructed from fabric, which can lend a
softer edge to a bedroom, and clothing envelopes and suit covers can
neatly hide away and protect all those excess clothes.

YOU WILL NEED:
- FABRIC OF
  YOUR CHOICE
- THREAD
- SEWING MACHINE
- SCISSORS
- PINKING SHEARS
- STEAM IRON
- PINS
- 2 x 31½-IN/800-MM
  LENGTHS OF CORD
- LARGE-EYE NEEDLE

PROJECT ONE
Drawstring bags

Drawstring bags are fantastically useful, and if you make yourself a set in pretty toning colors, you'll wonder how you managed without them. They make an attractive addition to the bedroom for make-up and jewelry storage, and can be used in the bathroom for cotton balls and cotton swabs. They are essential for keeping children's rooms tidy, too!

Make this drawstring bag in velvet for precious valuables, or a sturdy cotton-lined version with waterproof fabric for use on the beach.

HOW TO DO IT

This medium-size drawstring bag is very versatile, and is a good size for storing footwear or clothing. Take a ⅝-in/15-mm seam allowance throughout, and simply change the dimensions of the rectangles to make a bag that will match your exact requirements.

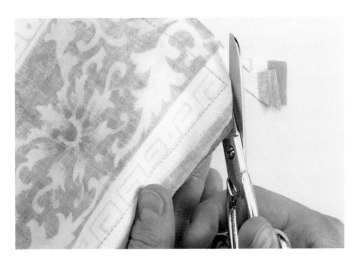

STEP 1 Cut two rectangles of fabric 24¾ x 15in/630 x 380mm. With the right sides facing, stitch the fabrics together along the long side edges and lower short edge, starting and finishing 140mm/5½in below the upper edges. Clip the corners.

STEP 2 Press the seam open, and press the side edges above the seam open. Neaten the seam with pinking shears. Press ⅝in/15mm under, then 2⅝in/65mm on the upper edges for the drawstring channels. Pin in place.

STEP 3 Stitch ¼in/6mm above the lower pressed edge then 1¼in/32mm below the upper pressed edge to form the drawstring channels. Turn the bag right side out.

STEP 4 Sew the end of an 31½in/800mm-long piece of cord to a large-eye needle and thread through the channel from the left-hand side of the front channel, and out of the right-hand side of the back channel. Repeat with another length of cord through the right-hand side of the front channel, emerging through the left-hand side of the back channel. Knot the cord ends together and adjust them so the knots are hidden in the channels.

YOU WILL NEED:
- **FABRIC OF YOUR CHOICE**
- **BATTING**
- **NEEDLE AND THREAD**
- **SEWING MACHINE**
- **SCISSORS**
- **PINS**
- **LARGE-EYE NEEDLE**
- **STEAM IRON**

PROJECT TWO
Lined baskets

Baskets come in all shapes and sizes, and a complementary lining adds a nice touch, as well as giving protection to the contents. Linings can be attached to the baskets with ties threaded through the weave of the basket, or tied around the handles. A lined basket is extremely useful.

Line a favorite picnic basket with cheerful plaid fabric, or line a Moses basket as a present for a newborn baby.

HOW TO DO IT

Choose light-to-mediumweight fabrics, and use a straight-side basket for best results. This lining for a picnic basket is padded to give some protection to breakables. The tie fastenings can be in a contrasting color if you wish.

STEP 3 With the right sides facing, stitch the short edges of the side panel together, taking a ⅝-in/15-mm seam allowance. Trim away the batting in the seam allowance. Press the seam open, taking care not to squash the batting flat. Press ⅜in/10mm under, then 1in/25mm on the upper edge. Stitch close to the inner pressed edge.

STEP 4 With the right sides facing, pin the side panel to the base, taking a ⅝-in/15-mm seam allowance and snipping the panel at the corners so the fabric lies flat. Stitch in place, pivoting the seam at the corners. Trim away the batting in the seam allowance, and neatly clip the corners.

STEP 5 Cut eight bias strips of fabric for ties 18 x 1½in/460 x 38mm. Fold lengthwise in half with the right sides facing and stitch the long edges, taking a ¼-in/6-mm seam allowance. Turn right side out with a large-eyed needle. Turn in the ends and press flat. Slipstitch the ends closed.

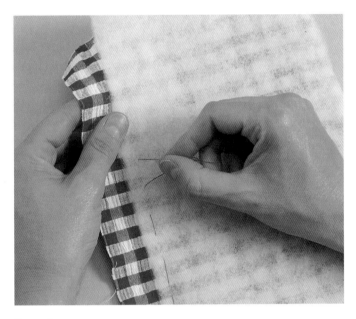

STEP 1 Measure the height of the inside of the basket, then measure the length of the sides at the top of the basket, again on the inside. Cut a strip of fabric for the side panel that is the length of the four sides plus 1¼in/32mm by the height measurement plus 2in/50mm. Cut a strip of 2oz/56g wadding that is the length of the four sides plus 1¼in/32mm by the height measurement plus ⅝in/15mm. Baste the batting to the side panel 1in/25mm below the upper edge.

STEP 2 Cut one square or rectangle of fabric and 2oz/56g wadding for the base that is the length of one side plus 1¼in/32mm by the length of an adjacent side plus 1¼in/32mm. Baste the fabric and batting base together along the outer edges.

STEP 6 Slip the lining into the basket and mark the position of the ties (usually one at each side of the corners). Remove the lining and match the center of each tie to the stitching line of the hem on the wrong side of the lining at the positions marked. Stitch back and forth a few times across the center of the tie to attach it securely.

YOU WILL NEED:

• FABRIC OF
  YOUR CHOICE
• PINS
• SEWING MACHINE
• THREAD
• PINKING SHEARS
• TOOL COMPASS
• PAPER
• SCISSORS
• LARGE-EYE NEEDLE
• 2 x 5FT 8IN/1760MM
  LENGTHS OF CORD
• STEAM IRON

PROJECT THREE

Spare comforter bolster bag

S pare comforters never seem to have a home of their own, and often get packed away uncovered at the top of the airing cupboard, where they can get musty. Sew a simple bolster

bag to keep your spare bedding tidy and clean. A set of bags could be made a feature of and hung up on a rail, or you could put them in a cupboard, or stow them neatly under the spare-room bed.

Bolster bags look good made in striped or plaid fabric, with a contrasting, colored cord tie.

HOW TO DO IT

Make the bolster bag from light-to-mediumweight fabric, bearing in mind that lightweight fabrics are easier to draw up than thick fabrics. Take ⅝-in / 15-mm seam allowances throughout.

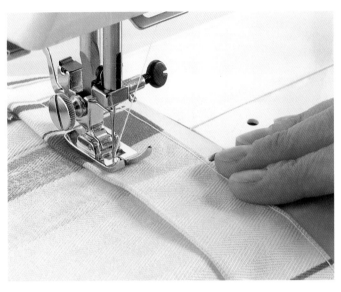

STEP 1 Cut two rectangles of fabric for the bolster 4ft 2in x 2ft 2in/ 1270 x 660mm. Pin the bolsters together along the long edges with the right sides facing, forming a tube. Stitch the side seams, leaving a 1-in/25-mm gap 2¼in/56mm below the upper edge for the drawstring channel.

STEP 2 Press the seams open and neaten them with pinking shears or a zigzag stitch. Press ¾in/20mm under, then 1½in/38mm on the upper edge for the drawstring channel, and pin in place. Stitch close to the upper edge, then 1in/25mm below the upper edge to form the channel.

STEP 3 To make a pattern for the base, use a tool compass to describe a 17-in/430-mm diameter circle on paper. Cut out the circle to use as a pattern to cut one base from fabric. Fold the base into quarters, and snip into the circumference at the folds. Fold the lower edge of the bag in half, and snip the fabric at the folds.

STEP 4 With the right sides facing, pin and stitch the base to the bolster, matching the snipped notches and the notches to the seams. Neaten the seam with pinking shears or a zigzag stitch. Turn right side out.

STEP 5 Using a large-eye needle, thread a 1760mm/5ft 8in length of cord through the channel, entering and emerging through the same hole. Knot the ends together, then fray the cord below the knot. Thread another length of cord through the other hole in the same way.

TIP
If you wish to trim the bag with ribbon, stitch one bolster seam first. Stitch ribbons or braid in bands across the piece, then stitch the other seam.

YOU WILL NEED:
- PATTERN PAPER
- SCISSORS
- FABRIC OF
  YOUR CHOICE
- NEEDLE AND THREAD
- SEWING MACHINE
- 43-IN/1090-MM
  ZIPPER
- ZIPPER FOOT
- PINS
- STEAM IRON

PROJECT FOUR

Clothes covers (plain)

Clothes covers protect clothing from snagging on other items, and keep it clean. Closely-woven natural fabrics keep dust out but allow the clothes to breathe. Plastic-coated fabrics are ideal for covers that are used for traveling, as they will protect against bad weather, but do not to store clothes in them for long periods, because the air cannot circulate.

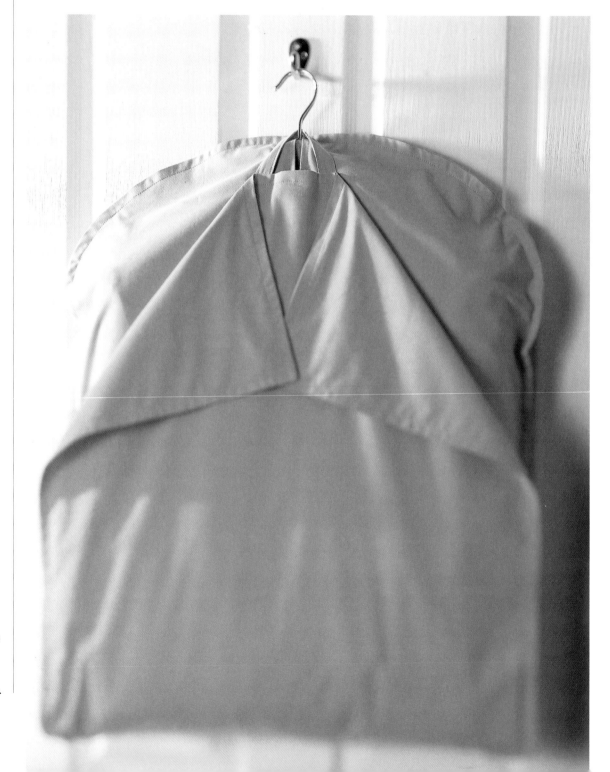

Protect special-occasion outfits with a smart set of clothes covers that can hang neatly at the rear of your wardrobe, or on the back of your door.

HOW TO DO IT

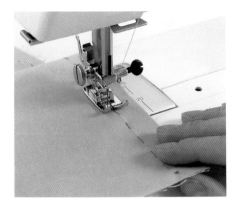

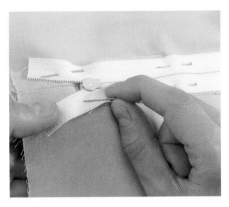

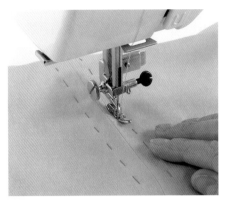

STEP 1 Refer to the diagram on page 85 to make a pattern for a cover on paper. Cut out the pattern, and use it to cut two fronts and one back (to the fold) from the fabric.

STEP 2 With right sides facing, baste the center front seam, taking a ⅝-in/15-mm seam allowance. Stitch the seam for ¾in/20mm at the upper end and 7in/178mm at the lower end, then press open.

STEP 3 With the front lying face down and starting at the base of the zipper, place a 43-in/1090-mm zipper face down centrally along the tacked seam. Pin and baste the zipper in position. A zipper cut from a continuous length will be unfinished at the top, so open the top of the zipper a little, and pin the top teeth under the seam allowances so the zipper does not slip off before stitching.

STEP 4 Using a zipper foot on the sewing machine, and with the front right side up, stitch the zipper in place ⁵⁄₁₆in/8mm from the basted seam, and across the base end of the zipper. Continue the stitching to the upper edge of the fronts. Remove the basting stitches.

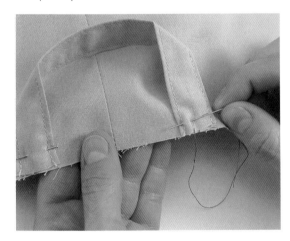

STEP 5 Cut a strip of fabric 6¾ x 2¼in/170 x 56mm for the hanging loop. Press 10mm/⅜in under along the long edges. Press the strip lengthwise in half and stitch close to both pressed edges. Pin and baste the ends 1¼in/32mm each side of the center front seam at the lower edge on the right side.

STEP 6 Open the zipper. Pin and stitch the front and back together with right sides facing, taking a ⅜-in/10-mm seam allowance. Clip the corners and snip the curves, then turn right side out and press. Topstitch ⅜in/10mm from the outer edges.

YOU WILL NEED:
• PATTERN PAPER
• SCISSORS
• FABRIC OF
  YOUR CHOICE
• NEEDLE AND THREAD
• SEWING MACHINE
• ZIPPER FOOT
• 38-IN/965-MM
  ZIPPER
• PINS
• PINKING SHEARS
• SCISSORS
• STEAM IRON

PROJECT FIVE

Clothes covers (gussetted)

This clothes cover has a generous gusset, making it deep enough to hold a suit or a few lightweight garments. Use a 38-in/965-mm zipper that has been cut from a continuous length.

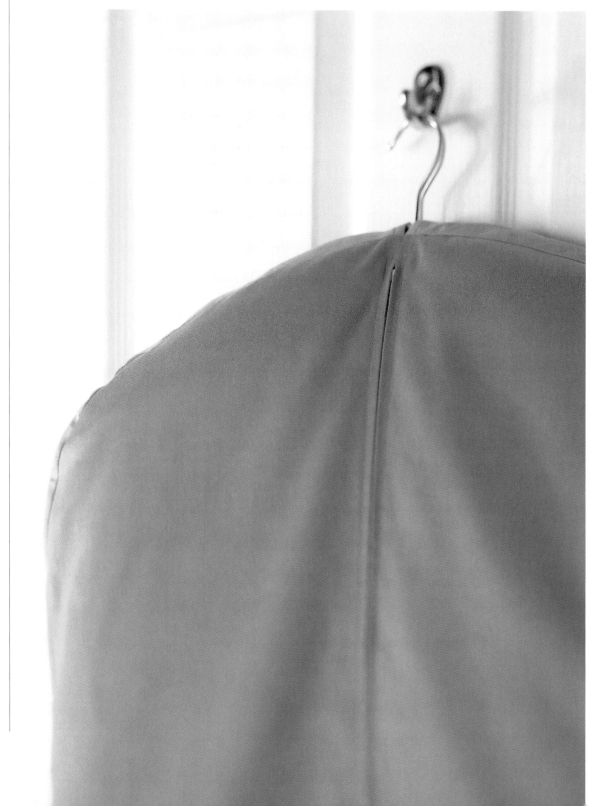

A gussetted clothes cover is ideal for more bulky items, or several items of clothing that you want to store away for a while.

HOW TO DO IT

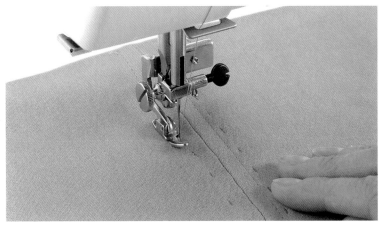

STEP 1 Refer to the diagram below to make a pattern for a cover on paper. Cut out the pattern, and use it to cut two fronts and one back (to the fold) from fabric. With the right sides facing, baste the center front seam, taking a ⅝-in/ 15-mm seam allowance. Stitch the seam for 1½in/38mm at each end, and press the seam open.

STEP 2 With the front lying face down, place a 38-in/965-mm zipper centrally face down along the basted seam. Pin and baste the zipper in position, pinning the top teeth under the seam allowances so the zipper does not slip off before stitching. Using a zipper foot on the sewing machine, and with the front right side up, stitch the zipper in place ⁵⁄₁₆in/8mm from the basted seam and across the ends of the zipper. Remove the basting stitches.

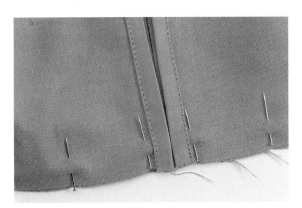

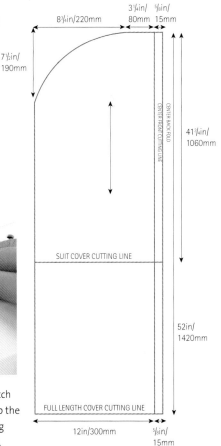

STEP 3 Measure the outer edge of one half of the front, ⅜in/10mm in from the raw outer edges. Cut two 3¼in/ 83mm-wide strips of fabric for the gusset that are the front measurement plus 1in/25mm. With the right sides facing, stitch one end of the gussets together to make one long length, taking a ⅜-in/10-mm seam allowance. Neaten the seam with pinking shears and press open. Press ¼in/6mm under, then ⅜in/10mm on the raw ends, and stitch close to the inner pressed edges.

STEP 4 Pin and stitch the gusset to the front with the right sides facing, with the ends of the gusset meeting end to end at the top of the center front seam, taking a ⅜-in/10-mm seam allowance. Snip the gusset at the corners so the fabric lies smoothly. Stitch a few times over the top of the center front seam to reinforce it.

STEP 5 Open the zipper, then pin and stitch the gusset to the back in the same way. Clip the corners and neaten the seams with a zigzag stitch or pinking shears. Turn right side out.

Diagram labels:

8¾in/220mm · 3⅛in/80mm · ⅝in/15mm

7½in/190mm

CENTER BACK FOLD / CENTER FRONT CUTTING LINE

41¾in/1060mm

SUIT COVER CUTTING LINE

52in/1420mm

FULL LENGTH COVER CUTTING LINE

12in/300mm · ⅝in/15mm

YOU WILL NEED:

- FABRIC OF
  YOUR CHOICE
- STEAM IRON
- PINS
- NEEDLE AND THREAD
- SEWING MACHINE
- 20-IN/510-MM
  LENGTH OF
  STRIPWOOD,
  1IN/25MM WIDE AND
  3¹/₁₆IN/4MM THICK
- SCISSORS
- 2 EYELETS
- EYELET PLIERS
- 2 HOOKS

PROJECT SIX

Shoe caddy

There is not always enough space to store shoes at the bottom of a closet, and a shoe caddy is a practical solution to the problem of freeing up space. It can be hung on a wall, or the inside of the closet door. Make the caddy from a hardwearing fabric such as canvas, heavyweight calico, or mediumweight denim, because shoes are quite heavy.

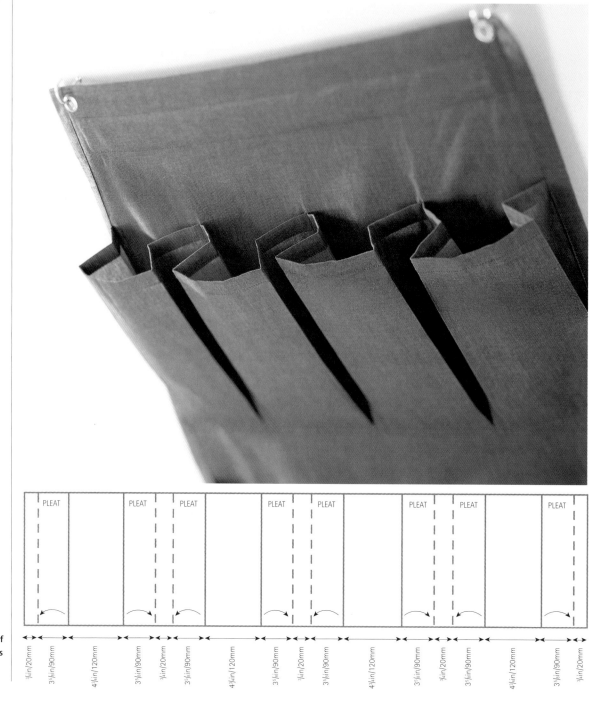

A sturdy shoe caddy will free up a lot of space at the bottom of your closet, and allows you to store your footwear neatly.

HOW TO DO IT

STEP 1 Cut three pocket strips from fabric 51 x 10⅝in/1300 x 270mm. Press ⅜in/10mm then ⅝in/15mm to the wrong side on the upper raw edges, and stitch close to the inner pressed edges. Fold the pleats along the solid lines to meet the broken lines. Pin and baste, then press the pleats.

STEP 2 Press ⅝in/15mm to the wrong side on the lower raw edge, and baste in place.

STEP 3 Cut a rectangle of fabric 39 x 22¾in/1000 x 580mm for the caddy. With right sides uppermost, lay the strips across the front, matching the short raw edges to the long edges of the caddy. Pin the lower strip ¾in/20mm above the lower edge. Pin the middle and top strip with a 2⅜-in/60-mm gap between all the pocket strips.

STEP 4 Baste the side and lower pressed edges of all the strips. Topstitch close to the lower pressed edges of the pocket strips, then ¼in/6mm above the first stitching.

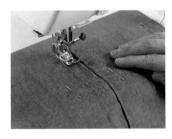

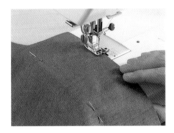

STEP 5 To form separate pockets, stitch between the broken lines of the pleats. Stitch back and forth a few times at the top of the stitching to reinforce the seam.

STEP 6 Cut a strip of fabric 22¾ x 4¼in/580 x 110mm for a facing. Press under ⅝in/15mm on the long lower edge. With right sides facing, stitch the facing to the upper edge of the caddy, taking a ⅝-in/15-mm seam allowance. Press the facing to the wrong side and topstitch close to the upper edge, then ¼in/6mm below the first stitching.

STEP 7 Stitch close to the lower edge of the facing, then 1½in/40mm above the lower pressed edge to form a casing. Slip a 20in/510mm-long length of 1in/25mm-wide and 3/16in/4mm-thick stripwood into the casing.

STEP 8 To bind the side and lower edge of the caddy, cut two straight 2⅜in/60mm-wide strips of fabric 39in/1000mm-long for the side edges, and one strip 24in/610mm long for the lower edge. Press under ⅜in/10mm on the long edges of the bindings, then press lengthwise in half with the wrong sides facing.

STEP 9 Slip one long edge of the caddy inside a side binding with the lower edges level. Turn under the end of the binding at the upper edge, and baste together through all the layers. Repeat on the other side edge. Stitch close to the inner pressed edge of the bindings.

STEP 10 Slip the lower edge of the caddy inside the lower binding with the binding extending at each end. Turn under the ends and baste through all the layers. Stitch close to the inner pressed edge of the binding. Remove the basting. Lay the batten centrally in the casing. Fix an eyelet 1in/25mm inside each top corner to hang on hooks.

YOU WILL NEED:
- FABRIC OF
  YOUR CHOICE
- SEWING MACHINE
- THREAD
- STEAM IRON
- PINS
- SCISSORS
- 2 BUTTONS
- NEEDLE
- 2 TOUCH-AND-
  FASTEN DISCS

PROJECT SEVEN

Tented closets

Freestanding wooden units are very cheap, and are great for storage purposes. The only drawback is that they are usually unattractive to look at, and everything in them is on display.

Make a streamlined fabric cover to hide the unit's contents, which rolls up and fastens with buttons to give access inside the unit. Fix a clothes rail inside if necessary.

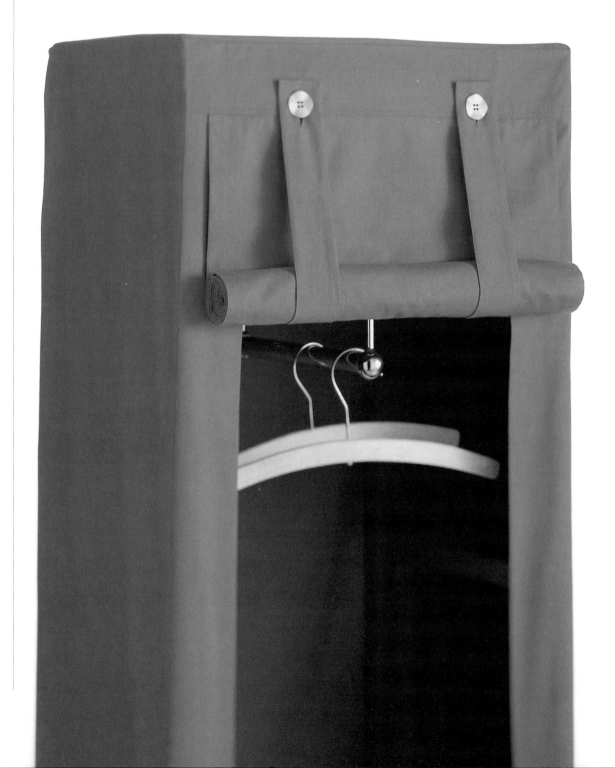

Conceal an unattractive unit behind a fetching fabric cover. This streamlined case fits the shape of the unit exactly.

HOW TO DO IT

Take a ⅝-in/15-mm seam allowance throughout.

STEP 1 Measure the width, depth, and height of the unit. For the door, cut two rectangles of fabric the height of the unit minus 1½in/40mm by the width of the unit. With right sides facing, stitch together along the side and lower edges. Clip the corners and turn right side out. Press and pin the upper raw edges together.

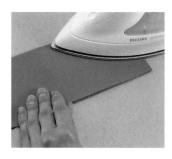

STEP 2 Cut two strips of fabric 18 x 4¾in/460 x 120mm for the straps. With right sides facing, fold the straps lengthwise in half and stitch down the long edges and across one end. Clip the corners, turn right side out, and press.

STEP 3 Work a buttonhole to fit your buttons ⅝in/15mm from the finished ends. Pin and baste each strap to the upper raw edge of the underside of the door 2¾in/70mm in from the side edges.

STEP 4 Cut two strips of fabric for the pediment that are the unit width plus 1¼in/32mm by 4in/100mm. With right sides facing, pin the upper edge of the door centrally to a long edge of one pediment.

STEP 5 For the front borders, cut two 6¾in/170mm-wide strips of fabric that are the height of the unit minus ¾in/20mm. Press the borders lengthwise in half with the wrong sides facing. Pin and baste the long raw edges together.

STEP 6 Matching the raw edges, pin the short upper edges of the borders to the pediment, overlapping the edges of the door. With right sides facing, baste the remaining pediment on top, sandwiching the door, straps, and borders. Stitch the upper edge. Turn the pediment right side out and press. Baste the raw edges of the pediments together. Topstitch the pediment close to the seam, then ¼in/60mm from the first stitching.

STEP 7 Cut a rectangle of fabric for the sides and back, which is the height of the unit plus 2in/50mm, by the width and twice the depth plus 1¼in/32mm. Join fabric widths if necessary with a flat felled seam. With right sides facing, stitch the front borders and ends of the pediment to the height edges, starting ⅝in/15mm below the upper edge. Press the seam open, and neaten the edges with a zigzag stitch.

STEP 8 Cut a square or rectangle for the roof that measures the width plus 1¼in/32mm by the depth plus 1¼in/32mm. With right sides facing, pin the roof to the upper edge of the unit cover, matching the pediment to the width edges. Stitch, pivoting the fabric at the corners.

STEP 9 Turn right side out and slip the cover over the unit. Pin up a double hem. Remove the cover, and sew a touch-and-fasten disc to the lower edge inside the front borders. Glue corresponding discs to the lower edge of the unit. Roll up the door. Sew the buttons to the pediment.

YOU WILL NEED:

- FABRIC OF
  YOUR CHOICE
- TRANSPARENT PLASTIC
- DRINKING GLASS
- SCISSORS
- PINS
- NEEDLE AND THREAD
- 1IN/25MM-WIDE
  READYMADE BIAS
  BINDING
- SEWING MACHINE
- SNAP FASTENER
- SMALL HAMMER

PROJECT EIGHT

Clothing envelopes

These indispensable clothing envelopes are ideal for storing summer beachwear when it is not in use in the winter, and underwear all year round. You don't have to stick to the dimensions shown here—make the envelopes as big as you need them to be.

Neat, plastic-fronted envelopes will keep their contents safe, free of dust, and easy to see at a glance. A snap fastening seals the envelope, and provides easy access when traveling, or for storing underwear, or T-shirts and sweaters in your drawers at home.

Choose plain or woven striped or plaid fabrics, as both sides of the fabric will be seen. The edges of the envelopes are bound with readymade bias binding.

Attractive, plastic-fronted envelopes can be used to store out-of-season clothes, or are very useful on holiday to hold swimwear, sarongs, and sunblock bottles.

HOW TO DO IT

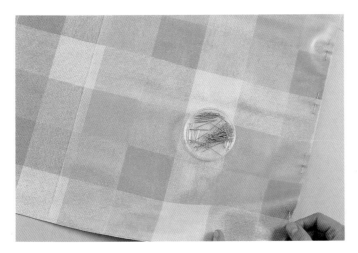

STEP 1 Cut a 16¼in/410mm square of fabric for the back, and a 16¼ x 12in/410 x 305mm rectangle of transparent plastic for the front. Place an upturned drinking glass on a corner of the back, and draw around it to make a curved corner. Cut out and repeat on each corner of the back. Pin the front to the back, matching the lower and side edges. Cut the lower front corners to match.

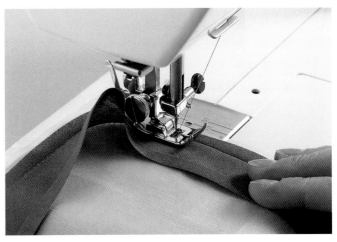

STEP 2 Open out one edge of 1in/25mm-wide bias binding. Turn one end under to start and pin to the outer edges of the fabric, overlapping the ends. Stitch along the fold line, taking a ⅜-in/10-mm seam allowance on the envelope.

STEP 3 Turn the binding to the back, enclosing the raw edges. Baste in place, then topstitch close to the pressed edges of the binding.

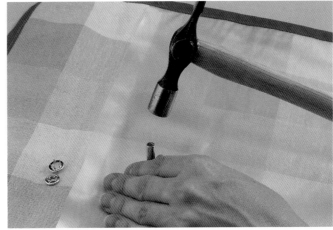

STEP 4 Following the manufacturer's instructions, attach a snap fastener centrally to the flap. Slip a few items of clothing inside to judge the position of the corresponding fastener. Remove the clothes and attach the snap fastener to the front.

YOU WILL NEED:
- PLAIN AND
  PATTERNED FABRIC
- PATTERNED RIBBONS
- NEEDLE AND THREAD
- SEWING MACHINE
- SCISSORS
- STEAM IRON
- 540-MM/21¼-IN
  LENGTH OF WOODEN
  BATTEN, 32MM/1½-IN
  WIDE

PROJECT NINE

Child's wall tidy

Encourage the children to tidy up with a jolly wall tidy for storing small toys and stationery. There are four generous, pleated pockets, and three patch pockets for smaller items. It is stiffened with a wooden batten at the top, and hangs from hooks on colored ribbons.

This brightly colored wall tidy might encourage your children to tidy their rooms! Let them choose the fabric for it.

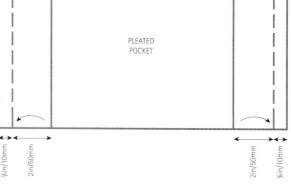

PLEATED
POCKET

⅜in/10mm   2in/50mm   2in/50mm   ⅜in/10mm

HOW TO DO IT

Take a ⅝-in/15-mm seam allowance throughout.

STEP 1 From plain fabric, cut two rectangles for the wall tidy 34⅝ x 22¾in/880 x 580mm. Cut four 1in/25mm-wide ribbons 10in/255mm long. Baste the ribbons in pairs to the short upper edge of one wall tidy on the right side, 3¼in/83mm in from the long side edges. With the right sides facing, stitch the wall tidies together, leaving a 8-in/200-mm gap 1in/25mm below the upper edge on one long side edge. Clip the corners, turn through, and press.

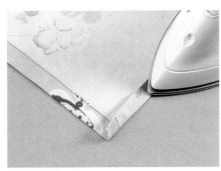

STEP 2 Cut four rectangles 13½ x 10¼in/ 342 x 260mm from three different fabrics for the pleated pockets. Center any design motifs. Press ⅜in/10mm, then ¾in/20mm to the wrong side on the upper raw edges. Stitch close to the inner pressed edges. Press ⅝in/15mm under on the side edges.

STEP 3 Fold the pleats along the solid lines to meet the broken lines (see diagram opposite). Pin and press the pleats. Press ⅝in/15mm to the wrong side on the lower edge.

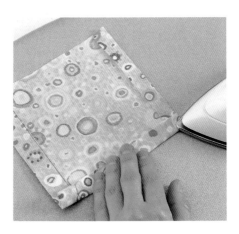

STEP 4 Cut three rectangles 7¾ x 6in/ 195 x 150mm from three different fabrics for the patch pockets. Center any design motifs. Press ⅜in/10mm, then ¾in/20mm to the wrong side on the upper raw edges. Stitch close to the inner pressed edges. Press ⅝in/15mm under on the side and lower edges.

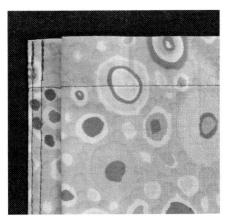

STEP 5 Arrange the pockets on the tidy, 1½in/38mm within the side and lower edges, and 5¼in/133mm below the upper edge. Topstitch close to the side and lower edges, then ¼in/6mm inside the first stitching. Stitch back and forth a few times at the hemmed edge of the pockets to reinforce them.

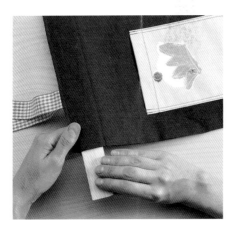

STEP 6 Stitch across the wall tidy ¼in/6mm, then 1¾in/45mm below the upper edge to form a channel. Insert a 1½in/38mm-wide wooden batten 21¼in/540mm long into the channel. Slipstitch the opening closed. Hang the tidy from hooks or a peg rail.

Index